MORE PROJECTS & PATTERNS:
A SECOND COLLECTION
OF FAVORITE QUILTS

NARRATIVES, DIRECTIONS, AND PATTERNS FOR 15 QUILTS

By Judy Florence

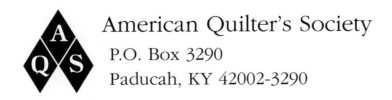

American Quilter's Society

P.O. Box 3290
Paducah, KY 42002-3290

ACKNOWLEDGMENTS

Thanks to...

My friends, who generously shared their artistic talents;
Dorothy Gilbertson, for her impressive Around the World crib quilt;
Marie Halmstad, for her inspiring creations, Blue Medley and Mexican Star;
Gladys Hayes, for her multicolored masterpiece, Double Wedding Ring;
Mary Mousel, for the graphic beauty of her Log Cabin;
Jane Noll, for linking the past with the present in Texas Stars;
Pat Simonsen, for her colorful Mixed-T baby quilt;

and to
The Clearwater Quilters, for their handsome fabric-rich Spools.

Jean Ray Laury's quotes on page 6 and 8 were first published in Quilter's Newsletter Magazine, *March 1990, and are reprinted here with the permission of* Quilter's Newsletter Magazine *and Jean Ray Laury.*

Portions of the Iroquois story and Rice Sack story first appeared in Quilting Today *magazine, and are included here with the permission of Patti Bachelder, Editor.*

Library of Congress Cataloging-in-Publication Data

Florence, Judy.
More projects & patterns: a second collection of favorite quilts; narratives, directions, and patterns for 15 quilts/by Judy Florence.
p. cm.
Includes bibliographical references.
ISBN 0-89145-994-4: $18.95
1. Quilting – Patterns. 2. Patchwork – Patterns. I. Title.
II. Title: More projects and patterns.
TT835.F62 1992
746.9'7 – dc20   92-35903
CIP

Additional copies of this book may be ordered from:
American Quilter's Society
P.O. Box 3290
Paducah, KY 42002-3290

@$18.95. Add $1.00 for postage & handling.

Dedicated with love to my parents
Leonard and Eilene Paulson
to commemorate their Golden Wedding Anniversary
November 3, 1940 - 1990

Table of Contents

"Quilts are commonly seen in the context of home, of loving care, of hour upon hour lavished on a humble object for another's pleasure. Even when the quilted work is hung on the wall and not intended for use, it carries the connotation of warmth, love, and care. The nostalgic connections cannot be eradicated. Part of the power and charm of a quilt lies in its original function: It was made to comfort another person. Overtones of that function remain and affect us. . . We could buy blankets, of course. We don't need quilts for physical warmth. We need quilts because they warm the hearts and souls of the makers as well as the users."

– Jean Ray Laury

INTRODUCTION

SOME THOUGHTS

A potpourri of impressive quilt patterns awaits you in *More Projects and Patterns: A Second Collection of Favorite Quilts*. This comprehensive book includes a variety of styles and techniques of general interest to all quiltmakers – designs with twinkling stars, swirling rings and reels, and colorful florals and plaids.

Although *More Projects and Patterns* is a continuation of *A Collection of Favorite Quilts: Narratives, Directions, and Patterns for 15 Quilts,* it is not just another pattern book. I have attempted to document several quilts and quiltmakers that have remained mostly unnoticed. I have also tried to relate the personal essence connected with each quilt: Who made it? Why was it made? What was the occasion? Is there a family connection?

Many of the quilts in this book moved from the hoop or frame directly to the cradle or bed. One beautiful scrap Spools quilt was completed by a local guild for a charity project and sold during a locally televised auction. Never entered in a quilt show or pictured in a periodical, this quilt had been nearly forgotten, and only sparingly documented.

The Trip Around the World crib quilt was more than 30 years in the making. Here is a project which was started for an infant son, set aside for personal reasons, and finished a generation later for an infant grandson, its completion an affirmation of the healing process of time.

Quilts that link generations – parent and child or grandparent and grandchild – are also highlighted. Several quilts were made specifically for grandchildren. Texas Stars includes pieces that were cut and pieced by a child's great-great-grandmother, and later assembled and quilted by the child's grandmother. The Double Wedding Ring quilt is a masterpiece of colorful fabrics pieced and quilted for a granddaughter's 16th birthday.

Nearly all the quilts have a very personal account associated with them. In the publication of patterns, the personal angle is usually sacrificed. I have tried to convey some sense of the long chain of humanity in quiltmaking by relating tidbits of the personal story of each quilt and its maker. It is hoped this will help us understand how quiltmaking extends both deep into the past and far into the future.

ADDITIONAL THOUGHTS

Three of the quilts in this book are of special importance to me. IROQUOIS was made for my son Matt. It represents my first attempt to incorporate important ethnic designs into a quilt. I made it more than 10 years ago, so it is not a new quilt. It has been displayed at local shows and festivals. I was reluctant to publish it because I felt its highly specialized designs had little "pattern potential" and because the pattern was so personalized.

I've changed my mind. Years of attending quilt shows and reading, hearing, and writing about quilts has convinced me that the "personal" story of the quilt is often not only the best part of the quilt, but also the most crucial. More often than not, the quiltmaker and the circumstances surrounding the making of the quilt have been tragically ignored.

When I began Matt's quilt, I researched written documents to increase my understanding of Iroquois culture and history. Several of the Native American designs used in the quilt were adapted from artifacts in New York state museums. For more than 10 years I had longed to visit these museums. Finally, one summer, we planned a family vacation to include a journey to see and study this part of Matt's cultural background. For me, it was a confirming experience that had little to do with the "publishability" of the pattern, but had plenty to do with the deeper process of creating a quilt for a loved one.

HEARTS ALONG THE PACIFIC RIM marks a family milestone – our 20th wedding anniversary. This is not such an earth-shaking event, but it did become an excuse for me to document, in fabric, the best 20 years of my life. The quilt represents more than just my husband and myself. Our children are also included. Small individual hearts mark the year of our marriage and the arrival and adoption of our sons. Each of the 20 fabrics recalls a time and a place we have visited – a relaxing family vacation to Hawaii, an excursion to Australia to meet my quilting pen pal, and ethnic explorations in David's Korean homeland. The appliquéing of each heart brought back many memories.

Certainly nobody will want to make a quilt just like mine. But surely there are hundreds of quiltmakers who would like to personally commemorate family milestones in fabric. A quilt cannot replace family genealogy records, but it can be another very expressive way to complement the written documents.

EXTRA FANCY U.S. NO. 1 reflects my current interest in using bags and sacks in quilts. Not many quilters get as excited about this as I do. Flour bags and feed sacks occupy a very humble place near the bottom of the pile of resources for quilts. On the list, they are down somewhere between leftover cuttings from sewing projects and cloth salvaged from rummage sale tables – a far cry from designer fabrics and imported cottons.

Sacks and bags may bring back uncomfortable memories of the Depression era, of inadequate resources, of having to wear underwear (or outerwear) made from sacks and bags, of "making do." It's the "making do" phenomenon that fascinates me. Today it continues to be done, only we don't hear about it as much, and certainly are less likely to publicize it. But now "making do" has a modern label called "recycling." And recycling is timely, maybe even fashionable, and certainly crucial.

Jean Ray Laury points out that "Patchwork has always been a humble art. The use of recycled fabrics does not detract in any way. It may define limitations but often adds an emotional dimension." The "spent" rice bags from our local Hmong refugee community bring both dimensions – recycled and emotional – to EXTRA FANCY U.S. NO. 1.

FIFTEEN FAVORITE QUILTS

A wide range of quilt styles and sizes is included in this book:

Small baby quilts, medium-sized lap/nap quilts, and large bed quilts. Several are appropriate as crib quilts:

Mixed-T Bow Tie Bears
Around the World

Several are appropriate for scrap mixtures:

Virginia Reel Double Wedding Ring
Texas Stars Spools

Most are pieced, but three appliqué quilts are included:

Hearts Along the Pacific Rim
Bow Tie Bears
Iroquois

There is also a decided emphasis on using plaid

fabrics in several of the designs. If you're willing to venture into the world of directional fabrics, consider these quilts:

Virginia Reel Spools
Cubic Plaid Bow Tie Bears
Evening Star

Some time-honored favorites are also included:

Log Cabin Eight-Point Stars
Double Wedding Ring

In format, this book is similar to its predecessor, *A Collection of Favorite Quilts*. Each chapter is divided into three sections: A narrative about the quilt; directions and diagrams; then patterns and quilting designs. The narrative relates the personal part of the quilt story, with a brief sketch about the quilt or its maker. The directions are outlined in six sections: For Starters (vital general information about the quilt), Supplies (fabric), Other Supplies (itemized), Ready to Work (making templates and cutting), Putting It Together (assembly), and The Finishing Touch (quilting and binding).

I have expanded the format in two ways. First is the inclusion of an Appendix, *Worksheets for Selected Quilt Patterns,* which includes grid sheets for sketching color and fabric options for nine of the pieced quilts. These worksheets are skeletal in nature, revealing only the piecing and setting lines. You can begin a quilt design by first sketching your ideas on a worksheet.

Some chapters also include bonus designs, extra variations or sets other than the one featured in the photographed quilt. The Mixed-T chapter includes nine additional "T" variations. The Blue Medley chapter has four secondary design alternatives. Three optional designs are illustrated in the Spools chapter. Six alternative set variations are given for the Virginia Reel.

With the help of the directions and patterns you can make any of the fifteen quilts. With the colorful photographs and the narrative you will gain a fuller appreciation of each quilt. Even if you decide not to use the patterns, you will at the very least be inspired by the uninhibited personal expression of each quiltmaker.

The Quilts

HEARTS ALONG THE PACIFIC RIM
(HEART APPLIQUÉ)
Quilt by the Author

HEARTS ALONG THE PACIFIC RIM

The making of quilts to mark milestones in life has been a long standing tradition in the quiltmaking world. Births, marriages, anniversaries – even departures and deaths have been recorded in the fabric and stitches of treasured quilts. HEARTS ALONG THE PACIFIC RIM marks such a milestone in our family – our twentieth wedding anniversary.

As the date of our anniversary drew near, I began to imagine ways in which I could record the 20 years my husband Dick and I and our sons Matt and David have shared together. A heart motif using favorite fabrics selected from my more than 16 years of quilting and fabric collecting seemed the natural choice.

A search through my boxes of fabric revealed several beautiful, large floral fabrics which I had not used – fabrics from a recent family vacation in Hawaii, from a family excursion to Australia to visit my quilting pen pal, a trip to David's homeland, Korea, and kimono fabrics from Japanese quilt friends and students. I discovered that I had a sufficient array of fabrics to make 20 hearts, each from a different fabric, each heart to represent a year of marriage.

For the background blocks I found special solids from my collection – a variety of hand-dyed fine cottons from a Japanese quiltmaker and soft cottons imported from China. I paired each floral with a compatible solid color.

The heart design is not difficult. It is ample in size, about 8" from side to side and top to bottom, appliquéd to a 12" background block. The pattern is large enough to ensure fairly easy appliqué – no sharp corners or fine points – one that I could complete in the few months before our anniversary date.

I used a freezer-paper appliqué method, cutting out the paper heart, pressing it to the wrong side of the floral fabric, cutting out the fabric heart with added turn-under allowance, pinning it to the background block, and appliquéing it in place. The method worked fine on my "test block" so I continued to cut and appliqué hearts – one, two, or three at a time, in various stages, washing and pressing all the fabrics as I progressed.

In the early stages of appliqué I showed the hearts to my husband, Dick, explaining the choice and source of fabrics. He was quick to respond with the idea of a quilt with a "Pacific Rim" theme. The 20 florals included three

from Hawaii, six from Australia, nine from Korea, and two from Japan. A description of each fabric is given below. Refer to the photograph on the opposite page to identify each fabric, reading from top to bottom, left to right (like a book), beginning in the upper left corner:

1. Orchid – from Honolulu, Hawaii; purchased at a store in Chinatown.
2. Aquamarine – from Honolulu, Hawaii; purchased at the same store.
3. Rose – purchased in a fabric shop in Seoul, Korea; selected by my son David.
4. Floral/Leaf – recycled child's kimono fabric from Mariko Iwakoshi, a student in my quilting class.
5. Dark Blue –Yukata cloth from Japan.
6. Yellow – purchased at fabric shop in Seoul, Korea.
7. Aqua – purchased at fabric shop in Seoul, Korea.
8. Peach – from the personal fabric collection of my Australian pen pal, Pam Ractliffe, Bacchus Marsh, Victoria. Pam opened her suitcase of scraps and invited me to take anything I wanted. I responded to her generous offer by selecting a few unusual pieces which I have treasured and used in special projects such as this one.
9. Beige – purchased in a variety store in Cairns, Queensland, Australia.
10. Pink – from the Seoul, Korea, fabric store.
11. Teal – purchased in a variety store in Cairns, Queensland, Australia.
12. Pink Roses – from the fabric store in Seoul, Korea.
13. Flamingo – David selected this as his "favorite" from the hundreds of bolts in the Korean shop. He wanted me to buy enough to make a quilt for his bed. Not being a "flamingo" person, I resisted his request, and settled on a half-yard piece, to be used sparingly in special places.
14. Bush Memories – gift from Australian quiltmaker Deborah Brearley. "Bush Memories" fabric designed by Deborah includes a bush ant, moth, butterfly, gum leaf, and an Aboriginal art motif.
15. White Floral – purchased in a Cairns, Queensland, Australia variety store.
16. Floral – from the Honolulu, Hawaii, shop.
17. Roses – from the Korean fabric shop.
18. Leaves – from the Korean fabric shop.
19. Small Floral – from the Korean fabric shop.

19. Small Floral – from the Korean fabric shop.

20. Toucan – purchased in a Queensland variety store.

As a means of personalizing the quilt for our family, I added small appliquéd hearts to mark the first year of our marriage and the arrival of our children. Two hearts in the upper left-hand corner represent my husband and myself in our first year of marriage, 1970-71. The small heart in the block with the dark yukata cloth is for Matt, our son who was born, "arrived," and was adopted in 1975. The small heart in the lower right area is for our son David, who came to our home as a 7-year-old and was adopted in 1985. A special tiny heart in the upper right area marks the year of David's birth (1977) in Korea.

Seventeen of the hearts are quilted with concentric hearts that diminish in size. Three blocks – the orchid, the yukata cloth, and the toucan – are quilted to highlight prominent motifs. A combination of diagonal quilting lines and small hearts fill the background.

What began as merely an appliqué project with lots of pretty fabrics became something very special. I think of it as a gift to my family, a way of confirming in fabric what has transpired in 20 years.

Yes, I finished the quilt in time for our anniversary. As soon as it was finished, I packed it up and hauled or shipped it to several quilt shows. The response was positive. Each time I unpacked the quilt, additional wrinkles and crease marks appeared. I always felt better when it was out of the suitcase. So I steamed out the fold marks and hung the quilt on the wall where it belongs, brightening and personalizing our dining area.

Some people have asked if I have made provisions to add to the quilt for continued years of marriage, family additions, changes, etc. No, I haven't. HEARTS ALONG THE PACIFIC RIM represents the first 20 years. When another milestone is reached, I'll probably make another quilt.

HEARTS ALONG THE PACIFIC RIM

FOR STARTERS

The following list will help you enjoy a smooth start and steady progress in your work on the Twentieth Anniversary Hearts quilt. It contains a variety of general information about making the quilt:

- Wash and press all fabrics before you begin.
- Twenty bold floral prints are needed for the appliquéd hearts.
- The 20 background colors include a variety of light and medium solids that coordinate with the florals.
- Scant ¼" seams are recommended for the turn-under allowance on the appliquéd hearts.
- Use ¼" seams for piecing the blocks and borders.
- For the heart template and quilt stencils, use sturdy plastic, cardboard, or sandpaper, and be sure to note the grain line.
- Hearts Along the Pacific Rim requires hand appliqué. Use the method of your choice. (Instructions for a simple and dependable freezer-paper appliqué method are included in the directions for the Bow Tie Bears quilt on page 119).
- Twenty appliqué blocks are required (unless, of course, you are commemorating some other numerical milestone).
- Each appliqué block measures 12" square, finished. The border is 3" wide.
- The finished size for Hearts Along the Pacific Rim is 54" x 66".

SUPPLIES

Use 44"/45" wide cotton or cotton/ polyester blends.

Quilt Top:

Bold Floral Prints: ⅜ yard each of 20 different fabrics; ¼ yard is sufficient if it is a "fat quarter" (18" x 22"). For scrap fabrics, the minimum size needed is a piece about 10" square.

Solids: ½ yard each of 20 different light and medium colors to match the bold florals. For scrap fabrics, the minimum size needed is a piece about 15" square.

Light Solid for Border (pale aqua): 2 yards

Binding: 1 yard of deep teal.

Backing: 4 yards of good quality unbleached muslin.

Batting: Use a 72" x 90" (twin size) bonded polyester batt.

OTHER SUPPLIES

- Iron
- Material for templates
- Freezer paper (optional)
- Marking pencils or soap chips
- Scissors (for paper and fabric)
- Rulers
- Thread for piecing
- Thread for appliqué, in colors to match the floral fabrics
- Pins
- Thread or safety pins for basting
- Quilting needles
- Two spools natural-color quilting thread
- Long straightedge
- Hoop or frame for quilting
- Appliqué scissors (optional)

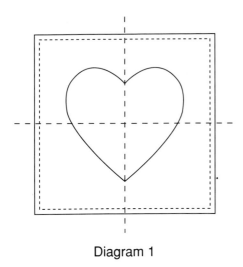

Diagram 1

READY TO WORK

TEMPLATES

Begin by making a sturdy template of the heart pattern on page 17. One-half of the pattern is given. It must be folded at the broken line to get the full heart-shape. A clear plastic template will be helpful in viewing and selecting design areas on the fabric. Mark the grain line on the template. Note that a scant ¼" turn-under allowance must be added.

CUTTING

Begin with the bold floral fabrics. Cut a large heart from each fabric, adding the turn-under allowance all around.

Next, cut the background squares, each 12½" x 12½" including seams.

Each background square should measure at least 12½" raw edge to raw edge. It is recommended that background blocks be cut slightly larger and trimmed after the appliqué is completed. This extra tolerance will allow for any shrinkage resulting from the appliqué stitching and any raveling from routine handling.

Continue with the Light Solid border fabric. Cut the following (allowances for seams and mitering included):

Cut two side borders 3½" x 66½".
Cut two end borders 3½" x 54½".

PUTTING IT TOGETHER

APPLIQUÉ

Begin by pairing the floral hearts and solid background blocks. Locate the center of the block by folding the square in half vertically and horizontally. Lightly crease with a warm iron. Prepare the heart piece according to the appliqué method of your choice. A simple freezer-paper method (which was used for the pictured quilt) is described in the directions section of the Bow Tie Bears quilt on page 119.

All edges of the heart should be turned under. Place the heart on the background block, matching the center of the heart (dot) to the center of the background block, as in Diagram 1. Pin or baste in place.

Appliqué with small invisible stitches. Use thread that matches the heart fabric, changing colors if necessary. It will be necessary to clip into the seam allowance in the point at the top of the heart. Do this very carefully, clipping only to within two or three threads of the turn-under line.

Make a total of 20 appliquéd hearts.

Optional Small Hearts: Smaller appliquéd hearts may be used to mark events such as marriages, births, adoptions, etc. Patterns for the two

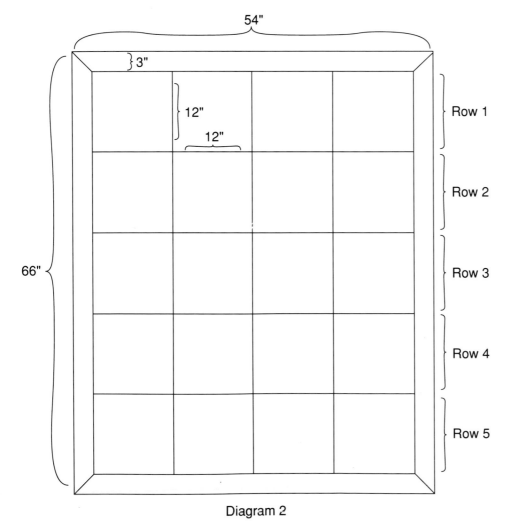

Diagram 2

smaller hearts used in the pictured quilt are included as optional templates.

ASSEMBLY

Refer to Diagram 2 for the general layout of the Anniversary Hearts quilt. Arrange the 20 blocks in five rows and four columns. Piece the four blocks in Row l in short vertical seams as shown in Diagram 3. Piece Rows 2, 3, 4, and 5 in a similar way. To complete the quilt center, join the five rows in long horizontal seams.

BORDERS

First, add the 3" side borders. Then stitch the end borders, mitering all corners.

THE FINISHING TOUCH

QUILTING

From the four yards of muslin backing fabric, cut two 2-yard lengths. Keep one intact (about 42" wide). From the other piece, cut two 9" widths. Join a 9" width to each side of the intact center panel. Press seams toward the outside.

Place the quilt backing right side down on a large, flat surface. Smooth the batting over it. Place the pressed quilt top over the batting, right side up. Pin or thread-baste the three layers together for quilting.

Use natural-color quilting thread to quilt the hearts, as illustrated in Diagram 4. Each heart contains five quilted concentric hearts. Clear plastic templates of each size heart will work well for marking the shapes within the appliquéd heart. Also, quilt two lines around each heart, one close to the appliqué and one about ¼" from the heart.

Use a straightedge and a washable marking pencil to mark the diagonal background lines, which occur at 1" intervals, as shown in Diagram 5. Two small hearts are placed between the blocks. One small heart is quilted into the border. Diagonal background lines

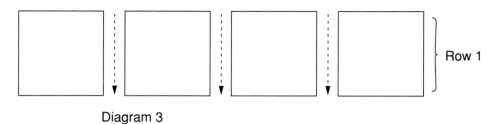

Diagram 3

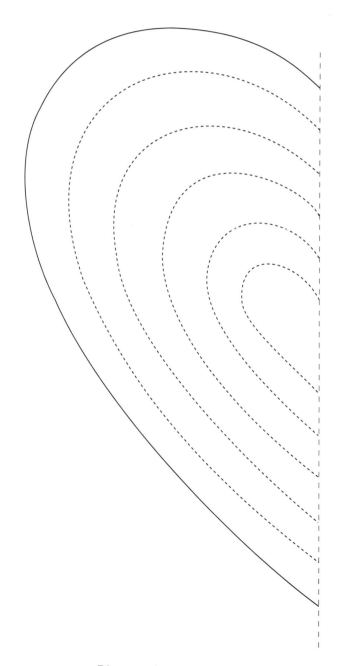

Diagram 4

Diagram 5

also continue into the border, as shown in Diagram 5.

BINDING

Trim the batting to ½" larger than the quilt top, to allow for filler in the binding. Trim the backing to match the top. From the one yard of deep teal binding fabric, make a 3" wide continuous bias. Fold the binding in half lengthwise, wrong sides together. Then attach it to the quilt front in a seam that penetrates all the layers. Turn the binding to the back and whipstitch it in place.

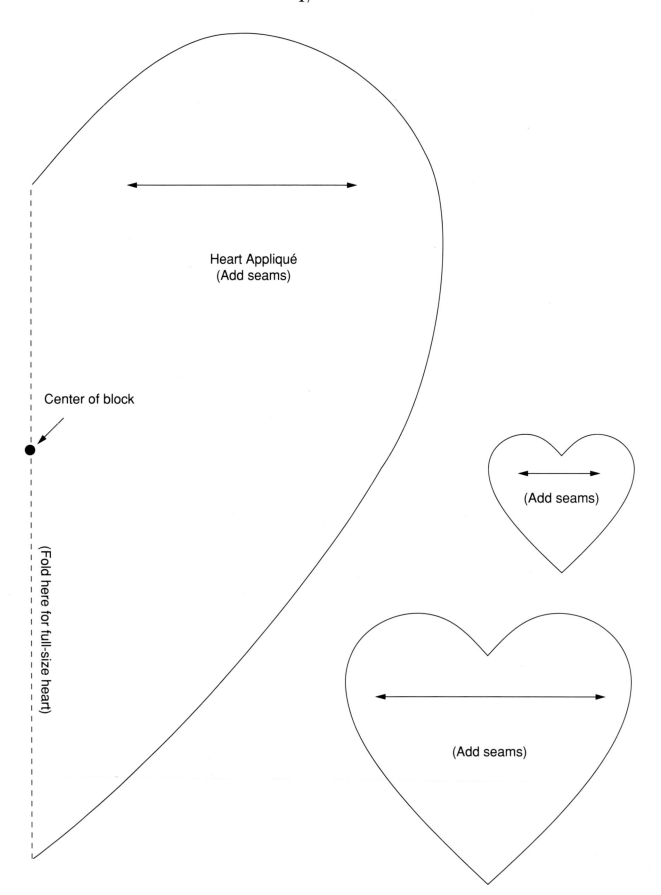

Heart Appliqué
(Add seams)

Center of block

(Fold here for full-size heart)

(Add seams)

(Add seams)

A NONDISCRIMINATION POLICY
(VIRGINIA REEL)
Quilt by the Author

A NONDISCRIMINATION POLICY

The Virginia Reel pattern is one of the best examples of how a very simple block can be set together into a very intricate design. Straight lines acquire a curved feeling and "whirlygigs" swirl across the surface. Early quiltmakers recognized the similarity between this pieced design and the Virginia Reel square dance where partners swing each other in graceful arcs.

You may know this pattern by other names – Snail's Trail, Monkey Wrench, Indiana Puzzle, or Interlocking Blocks. All are based on the simple "box-in-box" design. What lends the motion and curves is the way the fabrics are positioned in each box. An orderly spiral placement of fabrics, as opposed to concentric, and a direct set of the blocks result in the illusion of curves.

I've been on the lookout for Virginia Reel quilts for several years. My earliest inspiration came from an antique quilt pictured in a Dutton engagement calendar. A later inspiration was found at the Virginia Consortium of Quilters' "Celebration '90." Participants had assembled a pair of beautiful Virginia Reel quilt tops and presented them to the organizers of the event. Each quilt reflected a random blend of blue fabrics in a united gesture of appreciation.

My first Virginia Reel quilt was an exercise in combining plaids with large floral prints. The piece, entitled "Tokyo, Toronto, Seoul, Nairobi and the Amish Dry Goods Store," is pictured in the book *A Collection of Favorite Quilts: Narratives, Directions, and Patterns for 15 Quilts.* This Virginia Reel quilt is a continuation of print and plaid combinations. Here, the colors are more restricted in an analogous scheme of blues, greens, teals, and lavenders. However, the range of fabrics is wider, including stripes, plaids, bold florals, fine prints, and solids. Plaids and florals still play the dominant roles.

You may recognize some expensive English and Italian cotton florals. You may also recognize pieces from local fabric discount stores. When it comes to fabric-mixture quilts, I usually employ a nondiscrimination policy. If the fiber, weave, and weight are acceptable for piecing and quilting, it matters little to me if the fabric was 95 cents a yard or $14.95 a yard. The main difference is that I probably have three yards of the 95-cent fabric and only one-fourth yard of the $14.95 piece.

Several of the stripes and windowpane fabrics are from my grandmother's scrap bag. Some light prints are from Pam, my Australian pen pal. Lush Korean cottons intertwine with dime-store prints and leftover fabric for a man's shirt. Some of the blue/green solids are hand-dyed cottons from Japan, others from the Amish dry goods store.

An extension of pieced triangles is used at the upper and lower edges of the quilt. Arrangement of the triangles reveals the unusual two- and three-pronged shapes (incomplete whirlygigs) that move from the quilt center into the borders. Border lines appear more definite on the top and bottom, less so along the sides of the quilt.

It's fun to try different set variations with the Virginia Reel. At the end of the chapter, look for a special section with six direct sets – Traditional, Light and Dark, Vertical, Staggered, On Point, and Amplified. After you have pieced your Virginia Reel blocks, experiment with these sets to find the one that works best with your fabrics and colors. A plain worksheet for sketching the "box-in-box" format is included in the Appendix.

VIRGINIA REEL

FOR STARTERS

The following list will help you enjoy a smooth start and steady progress in your work on the Virginia Reel quilt. It contains a variety of general information about making the quilt.

- Wash and press all fabrics before you begin.
- A large variety of light and dark fabrics are needed, including fine prints, bold prints, plaids, and stripes.
- Dark solid colors are used in the outer edges of the quilt.
- All seams are ¼".
- For templates (patterns of the quilt pieces) use sturdy plastic, cardboard, or sandpaper, and be sure to note grain lines.
- Piecing may be done by hand or machine. For hand piecing, make the templates without seam allowances, and add them when marking and cutting the fabrics. For machine piecing, include the ¼" seam allowances on the templates.
- Twenty pieced Virginia Reel blocks are needed.
- Each pieced block measures a scant 12" x 12" square, finished.
- Pieced triangle extensions are added at the upper and lower ends of the central pieced blocks.
- A pieced outer border frames the design.
- The finished size for the Virginia Reel quilt is 56½" by 79¼".

SUPPLIES

Use 44"/45" cotton or cotton/ polyester blends.

Quilt Top:

Dark and Medium/Dark Prints: ¼ yard EACH of 20 fabrics, including both prints and plaids, in a mixture of blues, greens, teal, and beige, OR 20 pieces of scrap fabrics, minimum size about 12" square.

Light and Medium/Light Prints: Same as Dark and Medium/Dark Prints above.

Dark Solids (outer borders): ¼ yard EACH of six or more fabrics in a range of blue, teal, and green, OR six or more pieces of scrap fabrics, minimum size about 14" square.

Binding: 1 yard of Bright Blue.

Backing: 5 yards of good quality unbleached muslin.

Batting: Use a 72" x 90" bonded polyester batt.

OTHER SUPPLIES

- Iron
- Material for templates
- Marking pencils or soap chips
- Scissors (for paper and fabric)
- Rulers
- Thread for piecing
- Pins
- Thread or safety pins for backing
- Quilting needles
- Two spools natural-color quilting thread

- Thimble
- Long straightedge
- Hoop or frame for quilting

READY TO WORK

FABRIC KEY
L = Light Print
D = Dark Print
S = Solid

TEMPLATES

Begin by making templates of all six Virginia Reel pattern pieces. Mark the grain lines on each template. It is especially important to note and adhere to grain lines when cutting and piecing triangles. Note that there are five different sizes of right triangles. The grain line on the largest triangle is on the long side. The grain lines for the other four triangles are on the short sides. Adhering to the suggested grain lines will help maintain block stability during piecing. (Grain lines may vary in some of the large triangles in the photographed quilt. Some plaid and stripe fabrics were cut to create visual linear effect.)

Note that ¼" seams must be added on all sides of each template.

FABRIC PLACEMENT

Begin by pairing each of the 20 Light and Medium/Light (L) fabrics with the 20 Dark and Medium/Dark (D) fabrics, until all the fabrics are paired. The paired fabrics should be compatible, but do not necessarily have to be "coordinated." It is not necessary to have perfect matches in color or fabric style. The success of the design depends more on the interaction of light and dark fabrics in neighboring blocks.

Pin the paired light and dark fabrics together.

CUTTING

From EACH of the 40 light and dark print fabrics, cut the following pieces:

Template 1: Cut 2

Template 2: Cut 2
Template 3: Cut 2
Template 4: Cut 2
Template 5: Cut 2

From the leftover print fabrics, select several lights and darks to use in the pieced extensions and borders. From the Dark and Medium/Dark fabrics, cut a total of 15 triangles from Template 6, with the grain along the long side. Some of these triangles may be cut in duplicate and placed in pairs in the upper and lower extensions (see photograph for ideas). Also cut two triangles from Template 5 (note grain line) for the upper extension area.

From the Light and Medium/Light fabrics, cut a total of 19 triangles from Template 6 for the extension areas and borders. Also, cut two of Template 5 for the lower extension area.

Continue with the Solid (S) fabrics and cut 24 of Template 6, with the grain along the long side of the triangle. (**Note that the photographed quilt includes both solids and dark print fabrics in the outer border – another design option.)

PUTTING IT TOGETHER

BLOCK PIECING

Refer to the Virginia Reel illustration in Diagram 1. Collect the 20 light and dark pieces needed to complete one block. Place the pieces right side up on a flat surface, according to Diagram 1.

Begin by piecing the light and dark squares, as in Diagram 2.

Complete the center "four-patch" as in Diagram 3.

Attach small triangles (two light and two dark) on each side of the pieced center squares, according to Diagram 4.

Check to be sure that the light

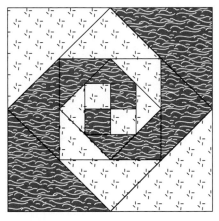

Diagram 1

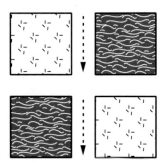

Diagram 2

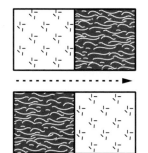

Diagram 3

Diagram 4

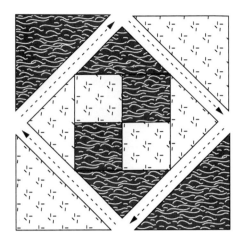

Diagram 5

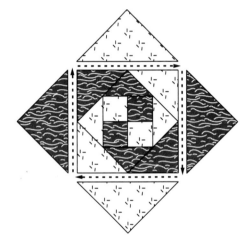

Diagram 6

Diagram 7

and dark fabrics are properly placed. Next, attach the medium triangles, as in Diagram 5.

Continue to add the large triangles, according to Diagram 6.

Add the outer largest triangles to complete the block as illustrated in Diagram 1.

Make a total of 20 Virginia Reel blocks.

ASSEMBLY

Lay out the blocks on a large, flat surface and arrange them according to your color and fabric preferences. Place them with the large triangles coming together to form dark and light "whirlygig" shaped clusters, as in Diagram 7.

Continue to arrange and rearrange with four blocks across and five blocks down, according to Diagram 8. Fabrics and blocks may be grouped by color or style.

After you have decided on block placement, begin piecing Row 1 in short vertical seams, according to Diagram 9. Piece Rows 2 through 5 in a similar fashion.

Next, join the rows in long horizontal cross seams, to complete the quilt center, referring to Diagram 8.

EXTENSIONS AND BORDERS

After the 20 blocks have been pieced together, lay the top on a large, flat surface. Position the remaining light and dark print triangles to make the upper and lower extensions and outer borders. Arrange the triangles to create a

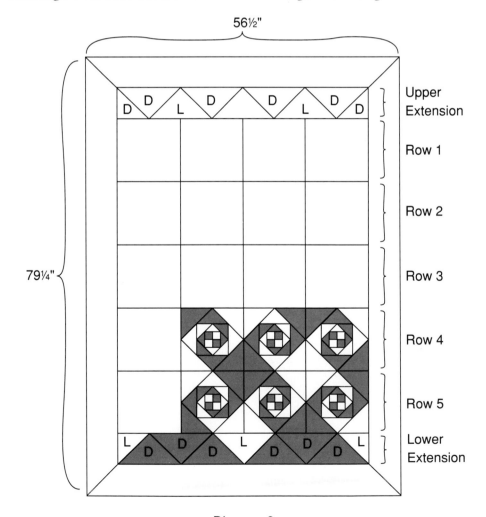

Diagram 8

pleasing continuation of the light and dark whirlygigs in the center. Then position the Dark Solid (S) large triangles in the outer area.

The corner triangles may be matched to give an illusion of a very large outer triangle. The photographed quilt includes some dark prints in the outer border. This is an optional arrangement. Make your design to reflect your preferences, feeling free to cut replacement triangles from the remaining fabrics, if necessary.

The upper extension is shown in Diagram 10. Collect the nine pieces: five large Dark (D) triangles, two large Light (L) triangles, and two medium Dark (D) triangles. Stitch them together carefully, as all seam edges are on the bias of the fabric.

The lower extension is shown in Diagram 11.

Collect the nine pieces: six large Dark (D) triangles, one large Light (L) triangle, and two medium Light (L) triangles. Stitch together.

Attach the upper and lower extension to the central Virginia Reel blocks.

The lower border is shown in Diagram 12. Stitch the four Light (L) Print triangles and five Dark Solid (S) triangles together as shown. Make a similar border for the upper edge of the quilt.

The right side border is shown in Diagram 13. Stitch four Lights, two Darks, and seven Solids together as shown. The left side border is shown in Diagram 14.

Attach the four border panels, mitering all four corners, to complete the quilt top (Diagram 8).

THE FINISHING TOUCH

QUILTING

From the 5 yards of muslin backing fabric, cut two 2½ yard

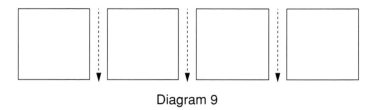

Diagram 9

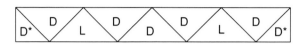

Diagram 10 (Upper Extension)
*Fabric may be matched with the adjacent Virginia Reel block

Diagram 11 (Lower Extension)
*Fabric may be matched with the adjacent Virginia Reel block

Diagram 12 (End Border) – make 2

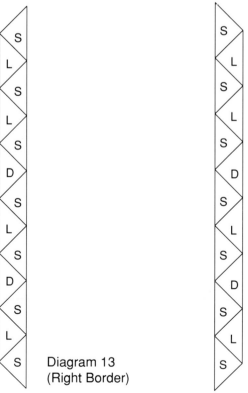

Diagram 13
(Right Border)

Diagram 14
(Left Border)

lengths. Keep one piece intact (about 42" wide). From the other piece, cut two 10" widths. Join a 10" width to each side of the intact center panel. Press seams toward the outside.

Place the quilt backing right side down on a large, flat surface. Smooth the batting over it. Place the pressed quilt top over the batting, right side up. Pin or thread-baste the three layers together for quilting.

Use a washable marker or soap chip and straightedge to mark the quilting lines suggested in Diagram 15. Use natural-color quilting thread to quilt along all marked lines.

Trim the batting to ½" larger than the quilt top, to allow for filler in the binding. Trim the backing to match the top. From the 1 yard of bright blue binding fabric, make 3" wide continuous bias binding.

Fold the binding in half lengthwise, wrong sides together. Then attach it to the quilt front in a seam that penetrates all the layers. Turn the binding to the back of the quilt and whipstitch it in place.

Diagram 15

DIFFERENT SET VARIATIONS FOR VIRGINIA REEL

Traditional

Light and Dark

Vertical

Staggered

On Point

Amplified

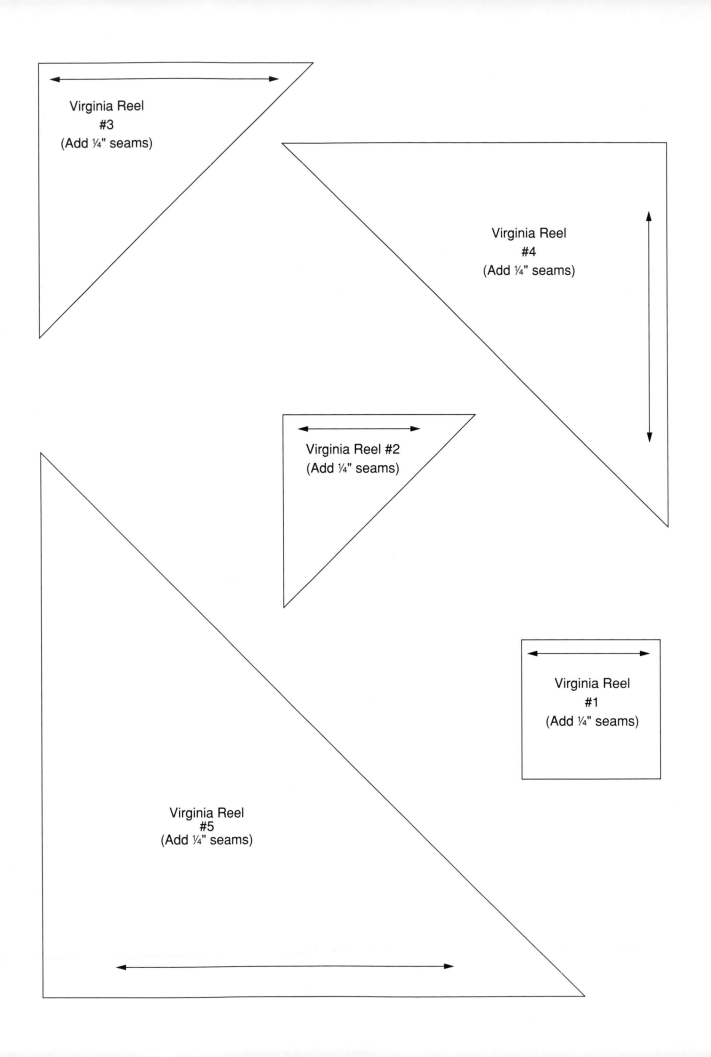

Virginia Reel
#3
(Add ¼" seams)

Virginia Reel
#4
(Add ¼" seams)

Virginia Reel #2
(Add ¼" seams)

Virginia Reel
#1
(Add ¼" seams)

Virginia Reel
#5
(Add ¼" seams)

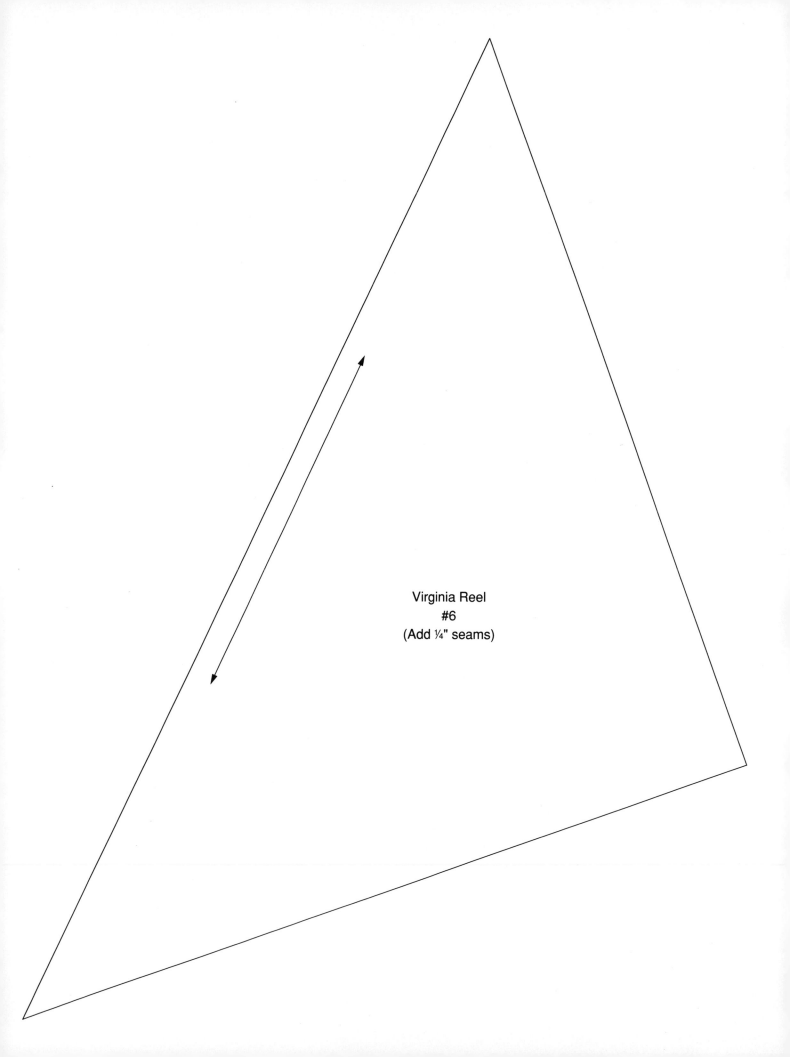

Virginia Reel
#6
(Add ¼" seams)

RHOMBOIDS, SQUARES, AND OBTUSE ANGLES
(CUBIC PLAID)
Quilt by the Author

RHOMBOIDS, SQUARES, AND OBTUSE ANGLES

If you're a quiltmaker who is not afraid to try designs that will turn heads and prompt questions, I suggest you try plaid fabrics. Most quilters of the 1970's and 1980's appear to have been operating according to an unwritten rule that plaids are not appropriate for quilts. On the contrary, research shows that quilters frequently used plaid fabrics throughout the past century – sometimes occasionally, sometimes intensively. Ginghams, checks, stripes, homespun, and plaids appear in pieced quilts. Page through any book that pictures or documents quilts from the past and you will note the presence and sometimes dominance of plaids. One North Carolina researcher notes that plaids were so abundant in some areas that they were used for quilt backs, as well as the fronts.

Until recently it seemed that plaids could not be found in quilt shops. They could be found in general fabric stores, but the average quiltmaker simply had not shown any interest in them, until recently. Today there is a growing number of high-quality cotton plaids available in quilt shops. Specially designed collections of cotton plaids and stripes have appeared on the market. And shop owners seem more willing to include a variety of plaids and stripes in their sea of fine prints and solids. Certainly this should be viewed as a welcome development.

For several years I have been gathering plaids of all styles and colors. This growing collection was the inspiration for my Cubic Plaid quilt, which includes 32 multicolored plaids featured in a "cubic" design.

Several plaids are from "fabric swapping" with students in my "Plaids – Who Said You Can't Use Them In Quilts?" workshop. Other special swatches came from pen friends Pam Ractliffe (Australia) and Mariko Iwakoshi (Japan) and New South Wales, Australia, quiltmaker Wendy Holland. Plaids from special shops as near as New Glarus and Land-O-Lakes, Wisconsin, to as distant as Greensboro, North Carolina, and Nairobi, Kenya, are included. Old shirting plaids and cuttings from home sewing days can also be found. The selections include even and uneven plaids, symmetrical and asymmetrical, and embellished (raised surface and embroidered) samples.

Each plaid square was cut "on grain" and set "on point," so the lines read diagonally on the quilt surface. The addition of four light pastel triangles around each square completes each block. The mixture of background triangles covers a rainbow range of colors – pink, yellow, green, aqua, blue, and lavender – gleaned from previous projects. (It's an undeniable fact that my fabrics keep reappearing. If you suspect you've seen a particular fabric before, perhaps even in this book, you probably have.)

The Cubic Plaid is a very basic design, simply a box-in-box or square-within-a-square. The cubic effect is achieved by staggering the rows by one-half block. This offset method creates the horizontal "zigzag" design. By turning the book 90-degrees, a "streak of lightning" effect can be viewed vertically.

First-time viewers frequently assume that Cubic Plaid is based on the 60-degree triangle, like the familiar Tumbling Blocks and its variations. It is not. All shapes and angles are based on the 45-degree right triangle. What this means technically is that we're talking squares, rhomboids, and right angles rather than hexagons, rhombuses, and obtuse angles. What it means practically is that it is totally straight-line piecing (no inset "pivot" seams), so it's easier to assemble.

The square-within-a-square format is an easy way to highlight a rich mixture of multicolored fabrics. Use the worksheet from the Appendix to plan your design. A search through your closet will probably reveal more plaids than you expected to find. If you're short on plaids, consider exchanging swatches with friends or investing in a few more pieces. You'll be surprised at what's on the shelves now that you know it's okay to use plaids in quilts.

CUBIC PLAID

FOR STARTERS

The following list will help you enjoy a smooth start and steady progress in your work on the Cubic Plaid quilt. It contains a variety of general information about making the quilt:

- Wash and press all fabrics before you begin.
- A large variety of plaid fabrics (up to 32 different fabrics) is required.
- A variety of light solid pastels are used for the background triangles.
- Scrap fabrics are suitable for the plaid squares and background triangles.
- All seams are ¼".
- For templates (patterns of the quilt pieces) use sturdy plastic, cardboard, or sandpaper, and be sure to note grain lines.
- Piecing may be done by hand or machine. For hand-piecing, make the templates without seam allowances, and add them when

marking and cutting the fabrics. For machine-piecing, include the ¼" seam allowances on the templates.

- Thirty-two pieced blocks are needed.
- Each pieced block measures 8" square, finished.
- Construction is by direct set of the blocks with an offset of a half block between rows.
- The dark inner border is 3" wide, the light outer border 2".
- The finished size for the Cubic Plaid quilt is 50" x 66".

SUPPLIES

Use 44"/45" wide cotton or cotton polyester blends.

Quilt Top:

Plaids: 32 different plaid fabrics. For scraps, the minimum size needed is a piece about 7" square. For new yardage, buy ¼ yard of EACH plaid fabric.

Light Solids: A variety of light pastels in light blue, light green, pink, and yellow. For scraps, the minimum size needed is a piece about 5" square. For new yardage, buy ⅜ yard EACH of light blue, light green, pink, and yellow.

Medium Solids: A variety of pastels (blue, green, aqua, and lavender). For scraps, the minimum size needed is a piece about 5" square. For new yardage, buy ¼ yard EACH of blue, green, aqua, and lavender.

Dark Blue (for inner border and binding): 2 yards.

Light Rose (for outer border): 2 yards.

Binding: Included in Dark Blue above.

Backing: 4 yards of good quality unbleached muslin.

Batting: Use a 72" x 90" (twin-size) bonded polyester batt.

OTHER SUPPLIES

- Iron
- Material for templates
- Marking pencils or soap chips
- Scissors (for paper and fabric)
- Rulers
- Thread for piecing
- Pins
- Thread or safety pins for basting
- Quilting needles
- Two spools natural-color quilting thread
- Thimble
- Long straightedge
- Hoop or frame for quilting

READY TO WORK

COLOR AND FABRIC KEY

P = Plaid
LP = Light Pink
LY = Light Yellow
LG = Light Green
LB = Light Blue
M = Medium Solid (Choice of blue, green, lavender, or aqua)
DB = Dark Blue
LR = Light Rose

TEMPLATES

Begin by making templates of the two Cubic Plaid pattern pieces – a square (Template 1), and a triangle (Template 2). Mark the grain line on each template. Note that ¼" seams must be added on all sides of each piece.

CUTTING

Begin with the Plaid (P) fabrics. Cut a large square (Template 1) from each plaid fabric. A total of 32 plaid squares are needed.

Continue with the Light Solid fabrics. Cut 30 triangles (Template 2) from EACH of the four colors: Light Pink (LP), Light Yellow (LY), Light Green (LG), and Light Blue (LB). If you are using scraps, cut a total of 120 triangles, evenly divided between the four colors.

Next, cut a total of 32 triangles

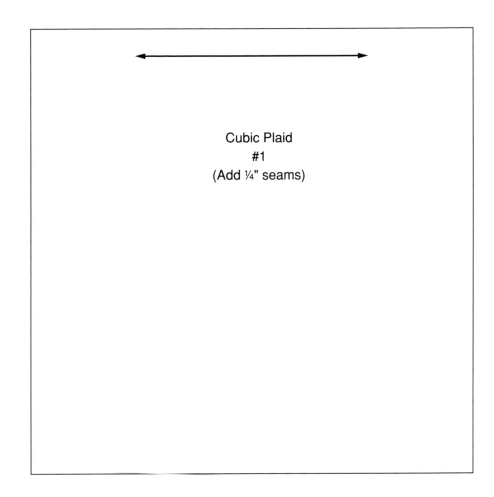

Cubic Plaid
#1
(Add ¼" seams)

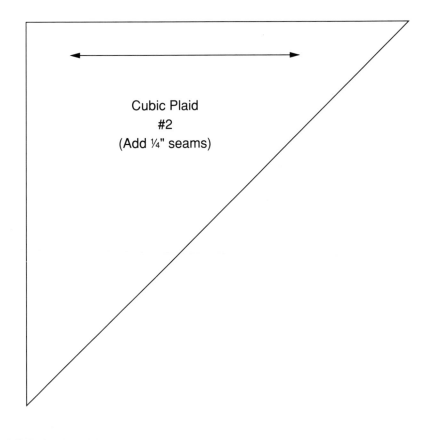

Cubic Plaid
#2
(Add ¼" seams)

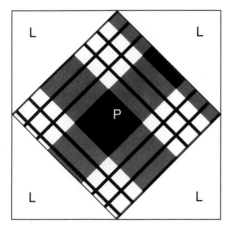

Diagram 1

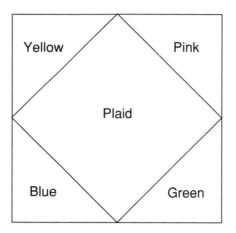

Diagram 2

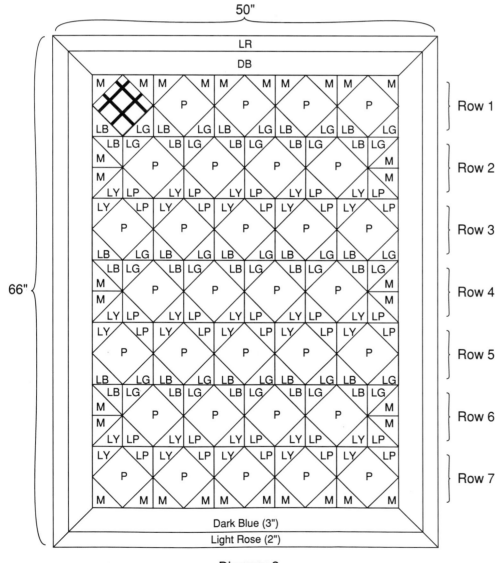

Diagram 3

from the Medium Solid (M) fabrics, divided evenly between blue, green, lavender, and aqua.

From the Dark Blue (DB) fabric, cut the following border pieces (allowances for seams and mitering included): Cut two side borders 3½" x 62½".

Cut two end borders 3½" x 46½".

Set the remaining Dark Blue (DB) fabric aside for binding.

From the Light Rose (LR) fabric, cut the following border pieces (allowances for seams and mitering included): Cut two side borders 2½" x 66½".

Cut two end borders 2½" x 50½".

PUTTING IT TOGETHER

COLOR PLACEMENT

The background colors in the Cubic Plaid are grouped to give a horizontal zigzag pattern that alternates between blues/greens and pinks/yellows. The medium solid colors (blue, green, lavender, and aqua) are placed in the outer edges (upper and lower) and side triangles that fill out the design.

Cubic Plaid is constructed by blocks. The basic block, a square-in-a-square, is shown in Diagram 1. The pieced blocks are set directly next to one another, with no latticework. The staggered or zigzag effect is created by the half-block offset between the rows. See Diagram 3 for a general layout of the quilt.

BLOCK PIECING

Refer to the Cubic Plaid block illustration in Diagram 1. Twenty-two of the blocks consist of a plaid square and four light triangles (one of each color), arranged in clockwise order of yellow, pink, green, and blue, as shown in

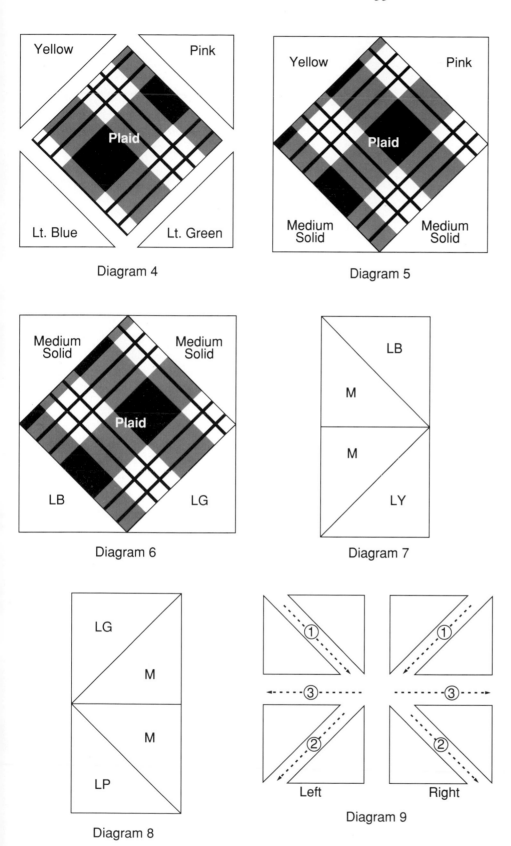

Yellow   Pink

Plaid

Lt. Blue   Lt. Green

Diagram 4

Yellow   Pink

Plaid

Medium Solid   Medium Solid

Diagram 5

Medium Solid   Medium Solid

Plaid

LB   LG

Diagram 6

LB

M

M

LY

Diagram 7

LG

M

M

LP

Diagram 8

Left   Right

Diagram 9

Diagram 2. (Blocks in the photographed quilt may occasionally vary from this format.)

Collect the five pieces needed to complete a block. Place the pieces right sides up on a flat surface, according to Diagram 2, with the four light triangles in clockwise order of yellow, pink, green, and blue. Stitch the triangles to the plaid square, as shown in Diagram 4. Make 22 blocks like this.

The remaining ten blocks are composed of both light and medium solid triangles. The five blocks at the bottom of the quilt consist of a yellow, a pink, and two medium solids (choose from blue, green, lavender, or aqua), as shown in Diagram 5. The five blocks at the top of the quilt consist of a light blue, a light green, and two medium solids (choose from blue, green, lavender, or aqua), as shown in Diagram 6. Six rectangular units are needed to fill out the sides of the quilt. Note that there are two unit designs. The left-side unit of the quilt is shown in Diagram 7. It is made with a light blue, a yellow, and two medium solid triangles of your choice. Collect the required triangles and make three left-side units. The piecing order for the side units is shown in Diagram 9.

The right-side unit is shown in Diagram 8. It is made with a light green, a pink, and two medium solid triangles of your choice. Make three of these right-side units, following the diagram.

ASSEMBLY

Arrange the 32 blocks according to the general layout in Diagram 3, noting that alternate rows are offset by one-half block. Position the six filler side-rectangle units. Check to be sure that the

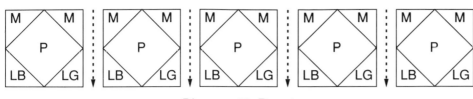

Diagram 10: Row 1

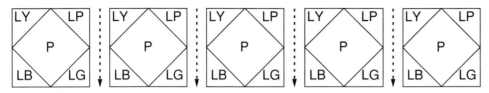

Diagram 11: Rows 3 & 5

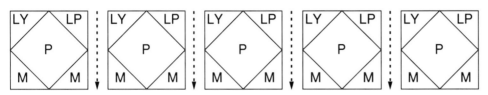

Diagram 12: Row 7

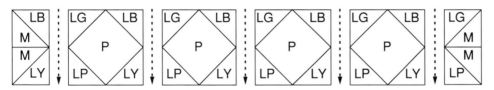

Diagram 13: Rows 2, 4 & 6

blocks are properly placed to create the zigzag background in blues/greens and yellows/pinks.

Piece the five blocks in Row 1 in short vertical seams, as shown in Diagram 10.

Piece Rows 3, 5 and 7 in a similar way. Note that Rows 3 and 5 are composed of blocks with all light background triangles, as shown in Diagram 11. Row 7 is composed of blocks with a pink, a yellow, and two medium solids, as in Diagram 12.

Rows 2, 4, and 6 are similar in make up, as shown in Diagram 13. Stitch the four blocks together. Attach a rectangle unit on each end, being careful to position the medium solids pointing toward the center. To complete the quilt center, stitch the seven rows together in long horizontal cross seams.

BORDERS

First, add the 3" Dark Blue (DB) border. Miter the corners. Next, add the 2" outer Light Rose (LR) borders.

Miter all corners.

THE FINISHING TOUCH
QUILTING

From the four yards of good quality unbleached muslin, cut two 2-yard lengths. Keep one intact (about 42" wide). From the other piece, cut two 6" widths. Join a 6" width to each side of the intact center panel. Press seams toward the outside.

Place the quilt backing right side down on a large, flat surface. Smooth the batting over it. Place the pressed quilt top over the batting, right side up. Pin or thread-baste the three layers together for quilting.

Use a washable marking pencil or soap chip and straightedge to mark the quilting lines suggested in Diagram 14. Use natural-color quilting thread. Quilt the borders with a continuation of the concentric diamonds and parallel lines from the center.

BINDING

Trim the batting to ½" larger than the quilt top, to allow for filler in the binding. Trim the backing to match the top. From the remaining Dark Blue (DB) fabric, make 3" wide continuous bias.

Fold the binding in half lengthwise, wrong sides together. Then attach it to the quilt front in a seam that penetrates all the layers. Turn the binding to the back and whipstitch it in place.

Diagram 14

A CROSS, AN "X," A DIAMOND, AND A SQUARE
(EVENING STAR)
Quilt by the Author

A CROSS, AN "X," A DIAMOND, AND A SQUARE

A growing number of beautiful quilts with plaid fabrics are being displayed in quilt shops and shows. With the increased availability of high-quality plaid fabrics and the strong likelihood that most quiltmakers have some plaid scraps stashed away in their collection, more quilters are using them in quilts and for good reasons. Plaids give a distinctive linear quality to quilts, adding a personality that cannot be conveyed with calico prints.

One of the best features of plaids is the potential for multiple design areas within a single fabric. Look closely at any plaid fabric and you will discover numerous color and design areas. By moving a window template across the fabric, multiple designs are revealed. The plaid fabric used in my Evening Star quilt was a natural choice for multiple designs. Only one plaid was used, but several design areas were selected for the center squares.

The multiple design areas concept is not new. Quiltmakers have used the method for fine and bold prints, juvenile prints, and border stripes. However, not many quilters have explored design areas on plaids.

An extra dividend with plaids is that they also give an illusion of elaborate piecing. In the center of each star I have highlighted designs which can loosely be described as a cross, an "X," a diamond, and a square. None of the centers are pieced. Each is an intact 6" square cut directly from the plaid. The four "design areas" were discovered by moving a 6" window template across the fabric and locating the designs. By positioning the template on edge, the square and cross were found. By positioning the template on point, the diamond and "X" were found. Several other designs, not included in Evening Star, were also found. Only four of the designs were selected and used in a repeat "sampler" format.

This technique might be described as "custom cutting" a plaid, a way of personalizing a project with "design-your-own" fabric. Taken one step further, you can also draft the size of your pattern to fit the design of your plaid. My plaid has a repeat of three colors at 2" intervals, so a 6" center square was the perfect size to display the plaid to the maximum. If the width or repeat of the plaids is greater, the pattern can be enlarged to accommodate the design. If the plaid is finer, the pattern size can be decreased.

The first quilt I made with plaid design areas was the Holiday Quick Quilt, published in the book *Award-Winning Quick Quilts*. Two contrasting areas on one plaid were highlighted in large squares set on point. At first glance, it looks as if two plaid fabrics were used. It is only one plaid with two design areas.

I made the Evening Star quilt expressly to highlight the plaid. The fabric was a two-yard length I purchased several years ago for a skirt. The skirt idea was soon abandoned and the fabric transferred to the box marked "plaids for quilts." Years later I resurrected the plaid and added two other fabrics – a deep cobalt blue solid for the Sawtooth Stars, and a light creamy solid for the background. The visual emphasis remained on the plaid, on the four design areas repeated in the stars.

The dark border was also cut from the plaid fabric. What appears to be pieced 2" squares is actually a crosswise strip of the darkest plaid line. Set into the border it gives an illusion of piecing.

Between the 12 scattered design areas and the crosswise strips for borders, my two-yard length of plaid was used nearly to maximum. All that remained was a handful of scraggly scraps and a few reject squares.

Venturing beyond the safety of fine prints and calicoes can be a slow process. Reluctance to use plaids in quiltmaking probably has to do with our earlier clothing construction experiences. With all the handsome new plaids now available, there's little reason to hold back. Once you recognize the eye-catching appeal of plaids, you're sure to welcome them into your quilt designs. Highlighting the multiple design areas of one favorite plaid is an easy way to get started.

EVENING STAR

FOR STARTERS

The following list will help you enjoy a smooth start and steady progress in your work on the Evening Star. It contains a variety of general information about making the quilt:

- Wash and press all fabrics before you begin.
- Three fabrics are suggested – a light solid, a dark solid, and a bold plaid.
- The success of the "sampler" effect in the center square of each star depends on the selection and placement of a wide repeating plaid.
- All seams are ¼".
- For templates (patterns of the quilt pieces) use sturdy plastic, cardboard, or sandpaper, and be sure to note grain lines.
- Piecing may be done by hand or machine. For hand-piecing, make the templates without seam allowances, and add them when marking and cutting the fabrics. For machine-piecing, include the ¼" seam allowances on the templates.
- Twelve pieced star blocks are needed.
- Each pieced block measures 12" square, finished.
- Construction is by direct set of the blocks, without latticework.
- The inner plaid border is 2" wide, the outer light border is 1" wide.
- The binding is 1" wide.
- The finished size for the Evening Star is 44" x 56".

SUPPLIES

Use 44"/45" cotton or cotton polyester blends.

Quilt Top:

Plaid: 2½ yards (The pictured quilt features a plaid with several repeating bands of color, each about 2" wide, in a range of blues and beiges.)

Light Solid (cream color): 4 yards (includes backing).

Dark Solid (cobalt blue): 1½ yards (includes binding)

Binding: Included in Dark Solid above.

Backing: Included in Light Solid above.

Batting: Use a 45" x 60" (crib size) bonded polyester batt.

OTHER SUPPLIES

- Iron
- Material for templates
- Lightweight cardboard for making window templates (two file folders will do)
- Clear plastic for see-through templates
- Marking pencils or soap chips
- Scissors (for paper and fabric)
- Rulers
- Thread for piecing
- Pins
- Thread or safety pins for basting
- Quilting needles
- One spool natural-color quilting thread
- Thimble
- Long straightedge
- 45/90-degree triangle
- Hoop or frame for quilting

READY TO WORK

FABRIC KEY
P = Plaid
L = Light Solid (cream)
D = Dark Solid (cobalt blue)

TEMPLATES
Begin by making templates of

the six Evening Star pattern pieces. Mark the grain lines on each template. Note that ¼" seams must be added on all sides of each piece. It will be helpful to make the large square pattern (Template 1) from clear plastic in order to view the plaid fabric through the template when selecting design areas.

CUTTING

Begin with the Plaid (P) fabric. Study the fabric to locate possible design areas. To assist with this, make several (four are suggested) "window" templates from the lightweight cardboard (file folders). Cut an 8" square from a folder section. Mark a 6" square inside the 8" square, leaving a 1" border all around, as in Diagram 1. Carefully cut out the 6" square, leaving intact the 1" border, as shown in Diagram 2. This "window template" can be placed directly on the plaid fabric to locate and isolate different design areas. Make four window templates.

Examine the plaid fabric for possible design areas.

Lay the fabric on a large, flat surface. Place the window templates on the fabric, moving and re-positioning the templates until suitable design areas appear in the "windows." Although the suggested grain line is along the sides of the square, you may rotate the window templates "on point" to discover additional design effects.

Note that half of the plaid design areas in the pictured quilt are from squares that were cut "on point." Try to locate as many design areas as possible, including both symmetrical and asymmetrical, on edge and on point, systematic and random. Note which designs you would like to include in the 12-block "sampler." The pictured quilt features four different design areas loosely described as a square, a

diamond, a cross, and an "X." Each design is repeated three times. You may use as many design areas as you like (up to 12), or a mixture of several selected designs (combinations of 2, 3, 4, and 6 work well). If only one design is selected, you may repeat it throughout all 12 blocks.

At this time you should also consider a choice for the plaid border. Select a plaid line (crosswise or lengthwise) that will make an effective border. If you choose a crosswise plaid, the border may need to be pieced to the necessary length. The suggested border width is 2", but this may be made wider or narrower to reflect the colors and widths of your plaid.

When you have settled on both border and center square choices, begin by cutting the four border pieces from the Plaid (P):

Cut two side borders 2½" x 48½" (seams included; pieced to length, if necessary).

Cut two end borders 2½" x 36½" (seams included; pieced to length, if necessary).

Next cut 12 large center squares using Template 1 (clear plastic) from the design areas of your choice. Be sure to add seams all around.

From Template 6, cut four small corner squares from a medium/dark portion of the Plaid (P) fabric.

Continue with the Light Solid (L) fabric. First, measure and cut off a two-yard length (72") of fabric. Label this to be used for the quilt backing and set it aside. From the remaining fabric (about two yards), cut two panels each 4" x 72", also to be used for the quilt backing. Label and set these aside.

Then cut the following pieces for the quilt top, beginning with the borders:

Cut two side borders 1½" x

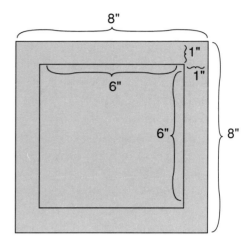

Diagram 1

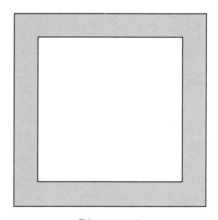

Diagram 2

52½" (seams included).

Cut two end borders 1½" x 40½" (seams included).

Cut 48 of Template 2 (large triangle).

Cut 48 of Template 3 (3" square).

Next, cut the following from the Dark Solid (D) fabric: Cut 96 of Template 4 (small triangle). Cut four of Template 5 (2" square).

Set aside the remaining Dark Solid (D) fabric for the binding.

Diagram 3

PUTTING IT TOGETHER

BLOCK PIECING

Refer to the Evening Star illustration in Diagram 3. Collect the 17 pieces needed to complete a block. Place the pieces right sides up on a flat surface, according to Diagram 3.

Begin piecing by joining two Dark (D) triangles to a large Light (L) triangle, as in Diagram 4. Make four of these. To make Unit I, add a Light (L) square on each end, as in Diagram 5. Make two of these.

For the center panel (Unit II), add a pre-pieced section on each side of the large center Plaid (P) square, as in Diagram 6.

To complete the block, attach a Unit I to the top and bottom of Unit II, as in Diagram 7.

Make 12 blocks.

ASSEMBLY

Arrange the 12 blocks in rows and columns, using the general layout in Diagram 8. You may prefer to rearrange the blocks, depending on how many repeated design areas you have selected.

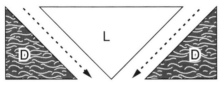

Diagram 4

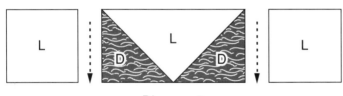

Diagram 5

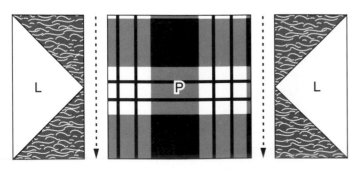

Diagram 6

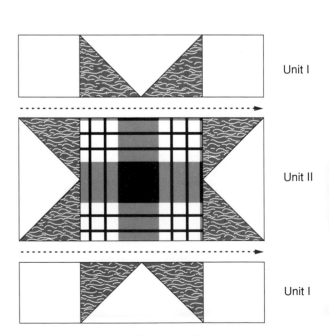

Unit I

Unit II

Unit I

Diagram 7

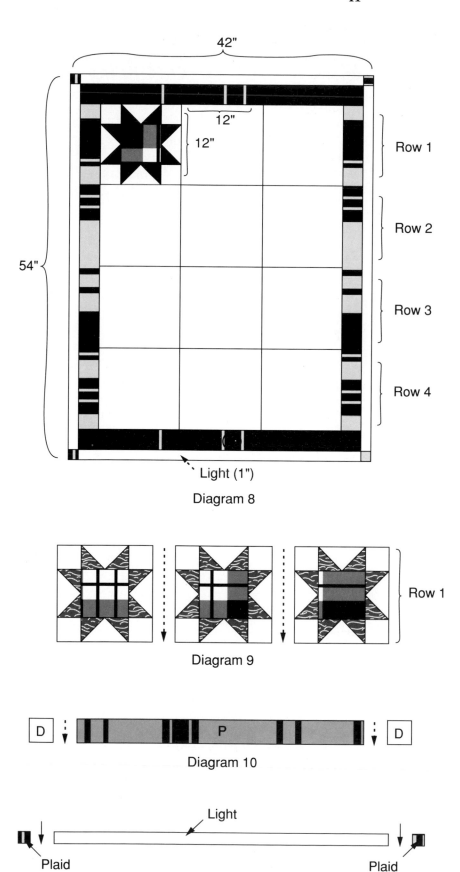

Diagram 8

Light (1")

When you have settled on the arrangement of your blocks, begin piecing Row 1 in short vertical seams, as shown in Diagram 9. Piece Rows 2, 3, and 4 in a similar way. To complete the quilt center, join the four rows in long, horizontal seams.

BORDERS

Begin with the inner 2" Plaid (P) border. First, join the two side borders to the pieced center, using Diagram 8 as a guide.

Next, attach a 2" Dark (D) square on each end of the plaid end borders, as in Diagram 10. Join the end borders to the pieced center.

Continue with the outer Light (L) border. Join the two side borders first, using Diagram 8 as a guide. Then attach a 1" Plaid (P) square on each end of the Light (L) end borders, as in Diagram 11. Join the end borders to the pieced center, to complete the quilt top.

Diagram 9

Diagram 10

Diagram 11

THE FINISHING TOUCH

QUILTING

Use the two-yard length and the two 4" x 72" panels of Light Solid (L) fabric that were previously cut and set aside for the quilt backing. Join a 4" panel to each side of the intact two-yard panel. Press the seams toward the outside.

Place the quilt backing right side down on a large, flat surface. Smooth the batting over it. Place the pressed quilt top over the batting, right side up. Pin or thread-baste the three layers together for quilting.

With a straightedge or large 45/90-degree triangle and a washable marking pencil, mark the quilting lines suggested in Diagram 12. Use natural-color quilting thread.

BINDING

Trim the batting to 1" larger than the quilt top, to allow for filler in the binding. Trim the backing to match the top. From the remaining Dark Solid (D) fabric, make 3" wide continuous bias.

Stitch the binding to the quilt front with the right sides together, in a seam that penetrates all layers. Press under ¼" on the other raw edge of the binding. Turn the binding to the back and whipstitch it in place.

Diagram 12

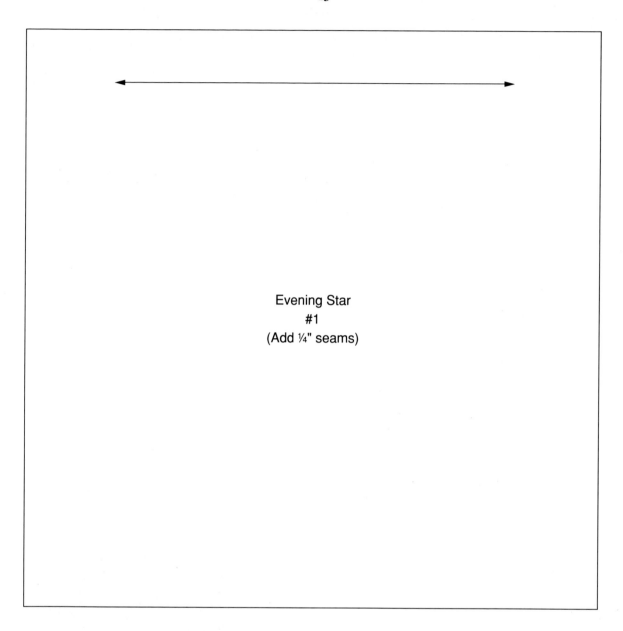

Evening Star
#1
(Add ¼" seams)

Evening Star
#2
(Add ¼" seams)

Evening Star
#4
(Add ¼" seams)

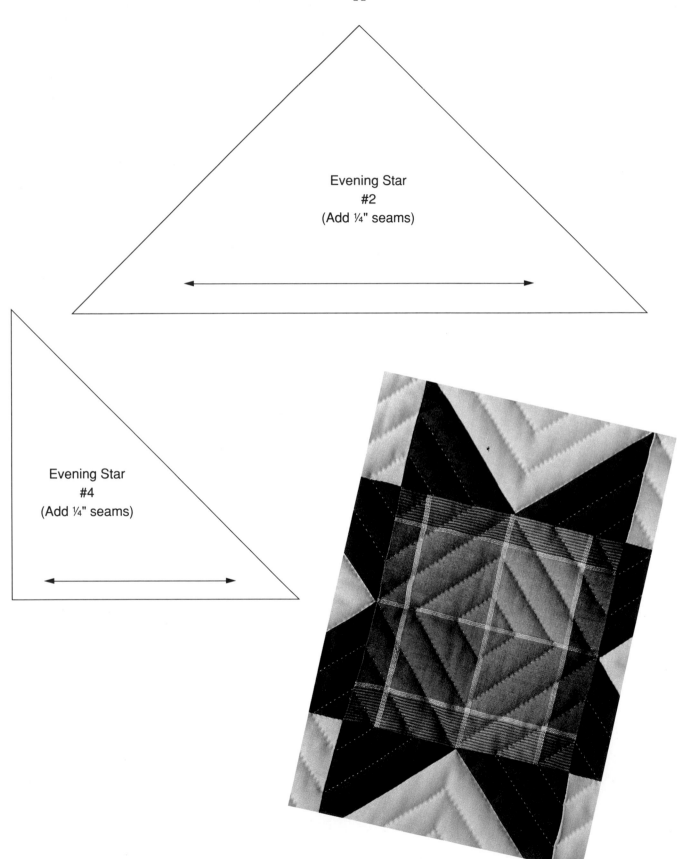

Evening Star
#6
(Add ¼" seams)

Evening Star
#3
(Add ¼" seams)

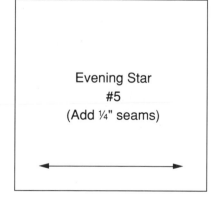

Evening Star
#5
(Add ¼" seams)

BLUE MEDLEY
(NINE PATCH STAR)
Quilt by Marie Halmstad, Eau Claire, Wisconsin

BLUE MEDLEY

A studied selection of fabrics and the formation of secondary designs make the BLUE MEDLEY quilt special. But what makes it extra special is that it was made by Marie Halmstad, who has been making quilts for over 60 years.

BLUE MEDLEY is a wall quilt designed at the request of Marie's daughter-in-law, Gail. Marie responded with several designs, each carefully sketched, graphed, and colored. One design was chosen, and Marie and Gail shopped together for fabrics in a quilt shop in a small west-central Wisconsin town. A mixture of six prints and solids were selected.

BLUE MEDLEY is made from one basic block, a Nine-Patch star, with a latticework of small squares. The primary block, as shown in Diagram A (PAGE 49), is sometimes called Doris' Delight. It closely resembles various traditional blocks such as 54-40 or Fight, Judy in Arabia, or Storm at Sea. Several references show slight alterations and placement variations associated with these names. But basically, it remains a Nine-Patch star.

The success of BLUE MEDLEY comes from the interaction of each block with the adjacent latticework. A larger four-pronged design, as shown in Diagram B, takes formation when the light background flows into the light fabric of the latticework and neighboring blocks.

A Shoo-fly-like design, as shown in Diagram C takes shape where the corners of four blocks and the pieced latticework come together. When the larger area around this "Shoo-fly" is considered, the most effective secondary design is revealed – a large polygon that gives an illusion of curved piecing, as shown in Diagram D. This many-sided figure (16 sides) creates an illusion of large light circles interlocked across the surface of the quilt. The result is an overall design of visual complexity.

From a geometric point of view, there are a couple of things that contribute to this illusion of curves. One is the scalene triangle (no sides equal) that forms the dark-blue star. The other is the isosceles triangle (two sides equal) in the light background fabric. Although these triangles cannot be labeled unusual, they are at least "less usual" with their sharp angles and uneven sides. They contribute decidedly to the "roundness" of the curved secondary designs. These triangles are somewhat more difficult to piece than the more familiar right triangles in other Nine-Patch stars such as the Ohio Star.

In addition to its captivating secondary designs, Marie's quilt also displays beautiful hand-quilting. Five original designs complement the piecing.

Marie is not a newcomer in the world of quilts. Another of her pieced quilts, Mexican Star, appears elsewhere in this book. One of her quick pieced achievements is published in the book *Award-Winning Quick Quilts*. Her first appliqué effort, a beautiful French Basket masterpiece, is included in the book *A Collection of Favorite Quilts: Narratives, Directions and Patterns for 15 Quilts*.

It was a pleasure to watch Marie as she progressed from one decision to the next, carefully considering and reconsidering the pattern, colors, fabrics, and quilting designs. BLUE MEDLEY has make its way from her sketch pad to the wall of her son and daughter-in-law's home. I'm sure we can look forward to more special quilts from this exceptional quiltmaker.

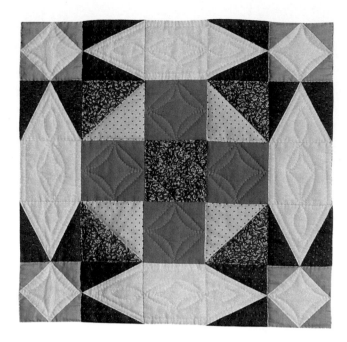

BLUE MEDLEY

FOR STARTERS

The following list will help you enjoy a smooth start and steady progress in your work on the Blue Medley quilt. It contains a variety of general information about making the quilt:

- Wash and press all fabrics before you begin.
- A minimum of six fabrics is required – three prints and three solids.
- All seams are ¼".
- For templates (patterns of the quilt pieces) use sturdy plastic, cardboard, or sandpaper, and be sure to note grain lines.
- Piecing may be done by hand or machine. For hand piecing, make the templates without seam allowances, and add them when marking and cutting the fabrics. For machine piecing, include the ¼" seam allowances on the templates.
- Fifteen pieced blocks are needed.
- Each pieced block measures 9" square, finished.
- The latticework is composed of blue, muslin, and rust 3" squares.
- The inner green border is 1½" wide; the outer blue border is 2" wide.
- The binding is 1" wide.
- The finished size for the Blue Medley quilt is 46" x 70".

SUPPLIES

Use 44"/45" cotton or cotton polyester blends.

Quilt Top:

Medium Blue Solid: 1 yard
Medium Green Solid: 2 yards
Muslin Solid: 4¼ yards (includes backing)
Dark Blue Print: 2⅛ yards
Rust Print: 1⅛ yards
Muslin Print: ¾ yard

Binding: Included in the Dark Blue Print above.

Backing: Included in the Muslin Solid above.

Batting: Use a 72" x 90" (twin size) bonded polyester batt.

OTHER SUPPLIES

- Iron
- Material for templates
- Marking pencils or soap chips
- Scissors (for paper and fabric)
- Rulers
- Thread for piecing
- Pins
- Thread or safety pins for basting
- Quilting needles
- One spool each of natural-color, light blue, and green quilting thread
- Thimble
- Long straightedge
- Hoop or frame for quilting

READY TO WORK

FABRIC KEY
B = Blue Solid
G = Green Solid
M = Muslin Solid
DB = Dark Blue Print
R = Rust Print
MP = Muslin Print

TEMPLATES

Begin by making templates of the six Blue Medley pattern pieces (1, 2, 3, 4, 5, and 6). Mark the grain lines on each template. Note that ¼" seams must be added on all sides of each piece. Also note that Template 5 (triangle) must be reversed for half of the pieces cut.

CUTTING

Begin with the Blue Solid (B) fabric. Cut 76 of Template 1 (large square).

Continue with the Green Solid (G) fabric. Cut the following borders (allowances for seams and mitering included):

Cut two side borders 2" x 65½".

Cut two end borders 2" x 41½". Then cut 60 triangles from Template 2 (tiny triangle).

Next, cut the following pieces from the Solid Muslin (M) fabric:

Cut two large panels each 25" x 75" for the quilt back. Label and set these aside.

Cut 38 of Template 1 (large square).

Cut 60 of Template 3 (large triangle).

Cut 15 of Template 4 (small square).

Cut the following border pieces from the Dark Blue Print (DB) fabric (allowances for seams and mitering included):

Cut two side borders 2½" x 70½".

Cut two end borders 2½" x 46½".

Then cut a total of 120 (60 in reverse) of Template 5 (small triangle). Note that half of these must be cut with the reverse template. Set aside the remaining (DB) fabric for the binding.

Cut the following pieces from the Rust (R) fabric:

Cut 24 of Template 1 (large square).

Cut 60 of Template 6 (medium triangle).

Last, cut 60 triangles from Template 6 from the Muslin Print (MP) fabric.

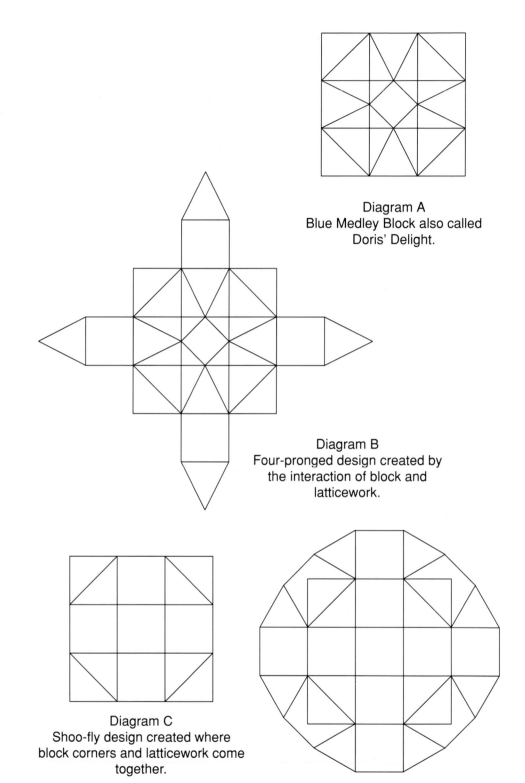

Diagram A
Blue Medley Block also called
Doris' Delight.

Diagram B
Four-pronged design created by
the interaction of block and
latticework.

Diagram C
Shoo-fly design created where
block corners and latticework come
together.

Diagram D
Larger area around Shoo-fly design can
become a large polygon.

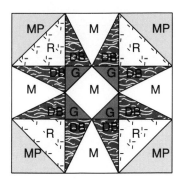

Diagram 1

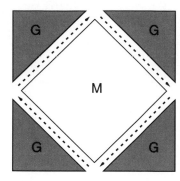

Diagram 2

PUTTING IT TOGETHER

BLOCK PIECING

Refer to the Around the Stars block illustration in Diagram 1. Collect the 25 pieces needed to complete a block. Place the pieces right sides up on a flat surface, according to Diagram 1.

Each block is composed of three smaller pieced units, designated as I, II, and III. Begin piecing Unit I by stitching Green (G) triangles on each side of the Muslin (M) center square, as in Diagram 2.

To complete Unit II, add Dark Blue (DB) triangles to the long sides of the Muslin (M) triangle, as in Diagram 3. Complete four of Unit II for each block.

To complete Unit III, stitch Rust Print (R) and Muslin Print (MP) triangles together, as in Diagram 4. Complete four of Unit III for each block. To assemble the center panel of the block, join a Unit II on

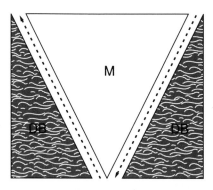

Diagram 3

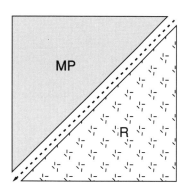

Diagram 4

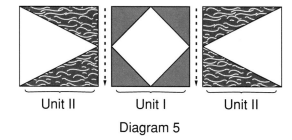

Unit II   Unit I   Unit II

Diagram 5

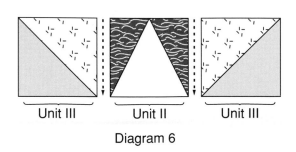

Unit III   Unit II   Unit III

Diagram 6

Diagram 7

opposite sides of the central Unit I, as in Diagram 5.

To assemble the outer panels, join a Unit III on opposite sides of a Unit II, as in Diagram 6. To complete the block, join the three panels, as in Diagram 7.

Make 15 blocks.

LATTICEWORK

Make a short lattice strip by joining two Blue Solid (B) squares on opposite sides of a Muslin (M) square, as in Diagram 8. Make 20 short lattice strips.

Make a long cross-lattice strip by joining 13 squares: four Rust Print, six Blue Solid, and three Muslin Solid, as in Diagram 9. Make six long lattice strips.

ASSEMBLY

Refer to the general layout of the Blue Medley quilt in Diagram 10. Assemble Row 1 by stitching three pieced blocks and four short lattice strips together, as in Diagram 11. Complete the other four rows.

Attach a long cross-lattice strip

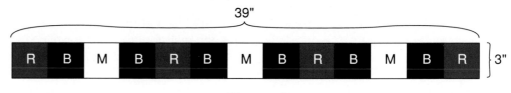

Diagram 9

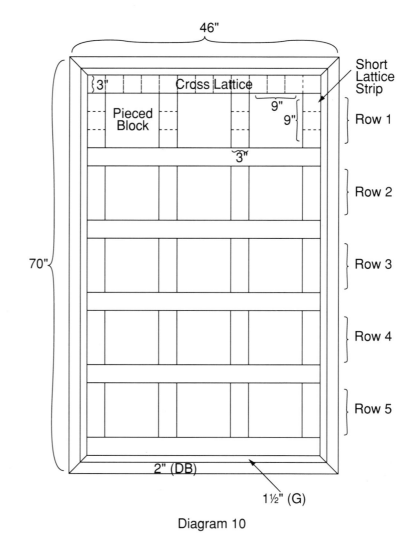

Diagram 10

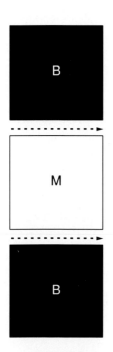

Diagram 8

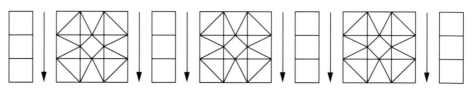

Diagram 11

between the five rows and also at the top and bottom, referring back to Diagram 10.

BORDERS

First add the 1½" Green (G) borders. Miter the corners. Next, add the 2" Dark Blue Print (DB) borders, mitering the corners, to complete the top.

THE FINISHING TOUCH

QUILTING

Stitch the two reserved Muslin (M) backing panels (25" x 75") together in a long seam. The finished backing piece will be about 50" x 75". Place the quilt backing right side down on a large, flat surface. Smooth the batting over it.

Place the pressed quilt top over the batting, right side up. Pin or thread-baste the three layers together for quilting.

Use a washable marking pencil and soap chip to mark the following quilting lines and designs, as suggested in Diagram 12:

• Quilt "in-the-ditch" around each triangle and square.

• Quilt Design A in each small center square.

• Quilt Design B in each large blue square.

• Quilt Design C in each large rust print square.

• Quilt Design D in the combined (elongated) muslin square/triangles area.

• Quilt Border Design E in the inner green border.

• Quilt Border Design F in the outer dark blue border.

Generally, use natural-color quilting thread on the Solid Muslin (M), Rust Print (R), and Muslin Print (MP) pieces. Use green quilting thread on the green and blue borders. Use light blue quilting thread on the large blue squares.

BINDING

Trim the batting to ½" larger than the quilt top, to allow for filler in the binding. Trim the backing to match the top. From the 1 yard of Dark Blue Print (DB) fabric, cut and piece 3" wide continuous bias strips to go around the quilt.

Fold the binding in half lengthwise, wrong sides together. Then attach it to the quilt front in a seam that penetrates all the layers. Turn the binding to the back and whipstitch it in place.

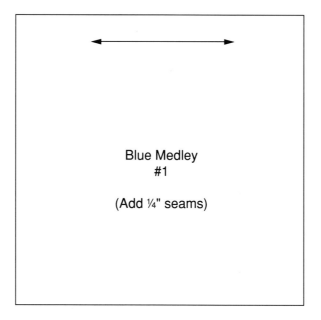

Blue Medley
#1

(Add ¼" seams)

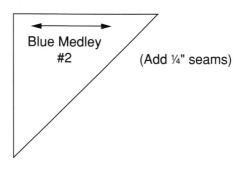

Blue Medley
#2

(Add ¼" seams)

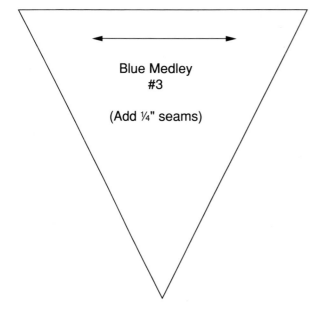

Blue Medley
#3

(Add ¼" seams)

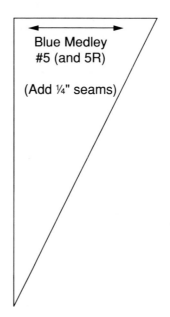

Blue Medley
#5 (and 5R)

(Add ¼" seams)

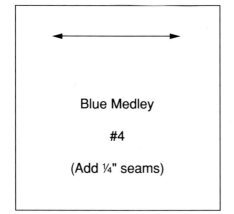

Blue Medley

#4

(Add ¼" seams)

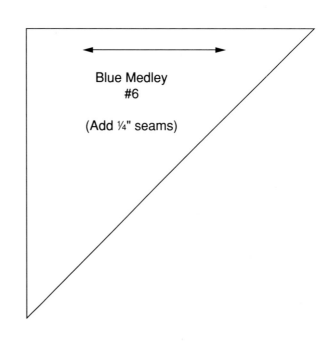

Blue Medley
#6

(Add ¼" seams)

Diagram 12

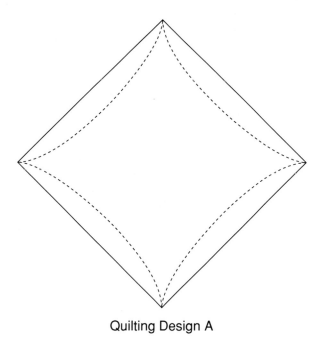

Quilting Design A

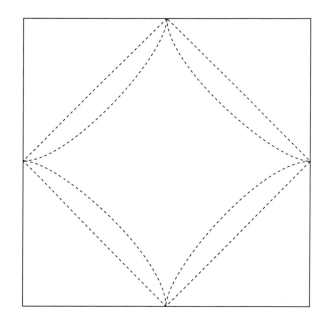

Quilting Design B

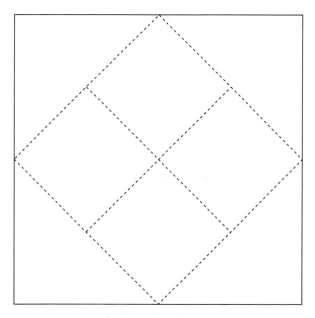

Quilting Design C

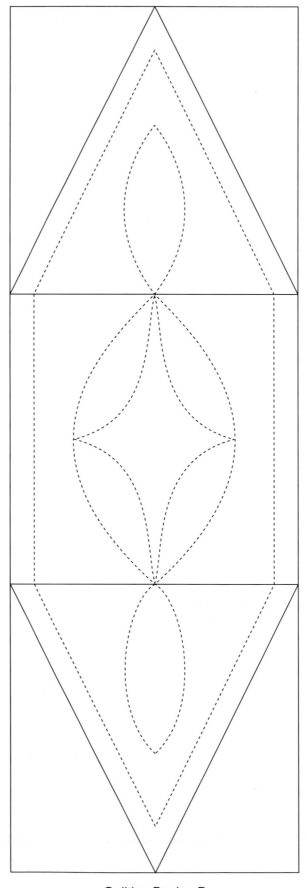

Quilting Design D

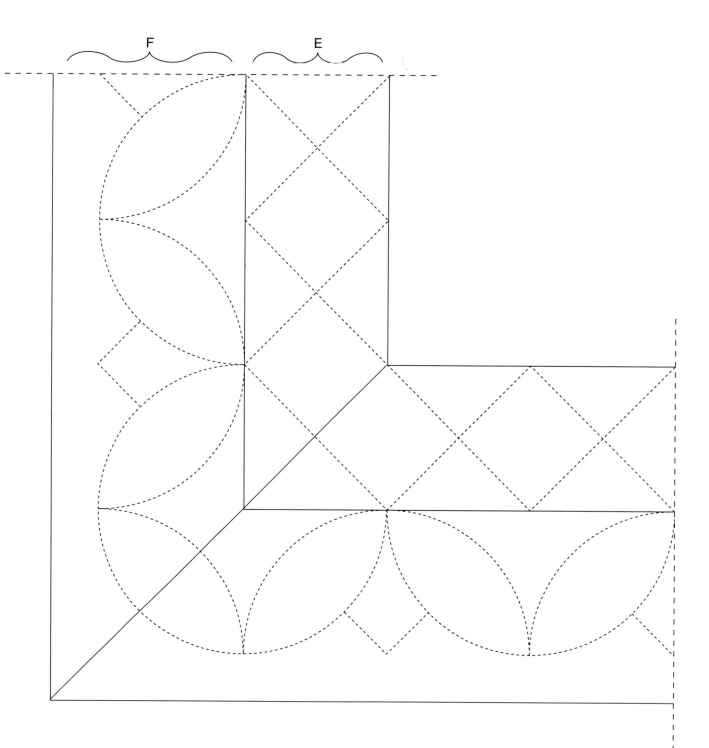

Quilting Designs E and F

MORE BEAUTIFUL THAN BEWILDERING
(MEXICAN STAR)
Quilt by Marie Halmstad, Eau Claire, Wisconsin

MORE BEAUTIFUL THAN BEWILDERING

Marie's Mexican Star is one of the more complex pieced patterns in this book. Although only a few templates and fabrics are required, the use of two unusual trapezoids and the direct set of the blocks give an illusion of complexity.

The striking graphic design of Mexican Star is accomplished by the omission of latticework. Several secondary designs take formation with the interaction of each block with its neighbors. Most obvious are the dark blue bands that criss-cross diagonally on the quilt surface. These elongated pieces would appear more like an "X" and less like a continuous gridwork if each block were interrupted with an alternate plain block or latticework.

The diagonal dark lines seem almost as strong visually as the star itself. In fact, the lines seem to cross in front of the star, making the rosy star appear to be in the background. Marie has further emphasized the diagonal effect by using the darkest fabric, which is also a directional fabric (a border print), for the elongated piece.

Close examination of the quilt detail shows that Marie also gave special attention to placement of the fabric. Each blue floral piece was carefully cut to give a medallion effect with the dark fabric as it moves from the small center square to the four corners. Even the corners where four Mexican Star blocks meet have a pieced garland of flowers.

Marie has placed the colors to reveal yet another secondary design, the suggested Nine-Patch which sits on point in the center of each block. This, of course, is not really a Nine-Patch. But it feels enough like a Nine-Patch that an enterprising quick-piecer could easily devise an alternative method for streamlined assembly of the center area.

Mexican Star can be assembled entirely with straight line piecing, i.e., no pivot or inset seams. Cutting and piecing need to be done in an orderly fashion, however, with proper attention to one template that must be reversed from time to time (the trapezoid that forms the star).

Ruby McKim describes the Mexican Star as "rather an intricate pattern to piece, but the effect when set together entirely of pieced blocks looks more beautiful than bewildering." You needn't be intimidated by all this jargon about intricate piecing, reverse templates, and secondary designs. Mexican Star requires only five templates and four fabrics. A worksheet for sketching your color and fabric options is included. The finished blocks are an ample 14", so your progress should be steady.

Mexican Star is just one in a growing and impressive list of quilts made by Marie. Another of her pieced designs, Blue Medley, appears elsewhere in this book. Her appliqué masterpiece SIXTY YEARS LATER AND STILL QUILTING is published in *A Collection of Favorite Quilts: Narratives, Directions, and Patterns for 15 Quilts*. We're certain to see many more lovely quilts from Marie.

MEXICAN STAR

FOR STARTERS

The following list will help you enjoy a smooth start and steady progress in your work on the Mexican Star quilt. It contains a variety of general information about making the quilt:

- Wash and press all fabrics before you begin.
- A minimum of five fabrics is required – three prints and two solids.
- All seams are ¼".
- For templates (patterns of the quilt pieces) use sturdy plastic, cardboard, or sandpaper, and be sure to note grain lines.
- Piecing may be done by hand or machine. For hand piecing, make the templates without seam allowances, and add them when marking and cutting the fabrics. For machine piecing, include the ¼" seam allowances on the templates.
- Twenty pieced blocks are needed.
- Each pieced block measures 14" square, finished.
- Construction is by direct set of the blocks, without latticework.

- The three borders are 4" inner (rose), 3" middle (muslin), and 4" outer (navy).
- The finished size for the Mexican Star quilt is 78" x 92".

SUPPLIES

Use 44"/45" wide cotton or cotton polyester blends.

Quilt Top:

Dark Blue Print: 2 yards
Medium Blue Print: ¾ yard
Rose Print: 2½ yards
Muslin: 2½ yards
Navy Blue: 2¾ yards
Binding: Buy an additional 1 yard of navy blue.
Backing: 6 yards of good quality unbleached muslin.
Batting: Use an 81" x 96" bonded polyester batt.

OTHER SUPPLIES

- Iron
- Material for templates
- Marking pencils or soap chips
- Scissors (for paper and fabric)
- Rulers
- Thread for piecing
- Pins
- Thread or safety pins for basting
- Quilting needles
- Two spools natural-color quilting thread
- Thimble
- Long straightedge
- Hoop or frame for quilting

READY TO WORK

COLOR AND FABRIC KEY
DB = Dark Blue Print
MB = Medium Blue Print
R = Rose Print
M = Muslin
N = Navy Blue

TEMPLATES

Begin by making templates of the five Mexican Star pattern pieces (1, 2, 3, 4, and 5). Mark the grain lines on each template. Note that ¼" seams must be added on all sides of each piece. Also note that Template 3 (trapezoid) must be reversed for half the pieces cut.

CUTTING

Begin with the Dark Blue Print (DB) fabric. Cut 80 of Template 5 (long template).

Continue with the Medium Blue Print (MB) fabric. Cut 100 of Template #4 (square).

Next, cut the following pieces from the Rose Print (R) fabric:

Cut two side borders 4½" x 78½" (allowances for seams and mitering included).

Cut two end borders 4½" x 64½" (allowances for seams and mitering included).

Cut 160 of Template 3 (trapezoid) (cut half of these [80 R] with the reverse template).

Cut the following pieces from the Muslin (M) fabric:

Cut two side borders 3½" x 84½" (allowances for seams and mitering included).

Cut two end borders 3½" x 70½" (allowances for seams and mitering included).

Cut 80 of Template 1 (large triangle).

Cut 160 of Template 2 (small triangle).

Cut the following border pieces from the Navy Blue (N) fabric:

Cut two side borders 4½" x 92½" (allowances for seams and mitering included).

Cut two end borders 4½" x 78½" (allowances for seams and mitering included).

PUTTING IT TOGETHER

BLOCK PIECING

Refer to the Mexican Star illustration in Diagram 1. Collect the 29 pieces needed to complete a block. Place the pieces right sides up on a flat surface, according to Diagram 1.

Begin piecing by joining a Rose (R) trapezoid to a small Muslin (M) triangle, as in Diagram 2. Add the large Muslin (M) triangle along the long edge of the trapezoid, as in Diagram 3.

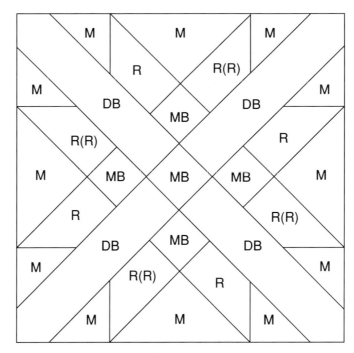

Diagram 1

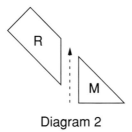

Diagram 2

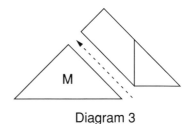

Diagram 3

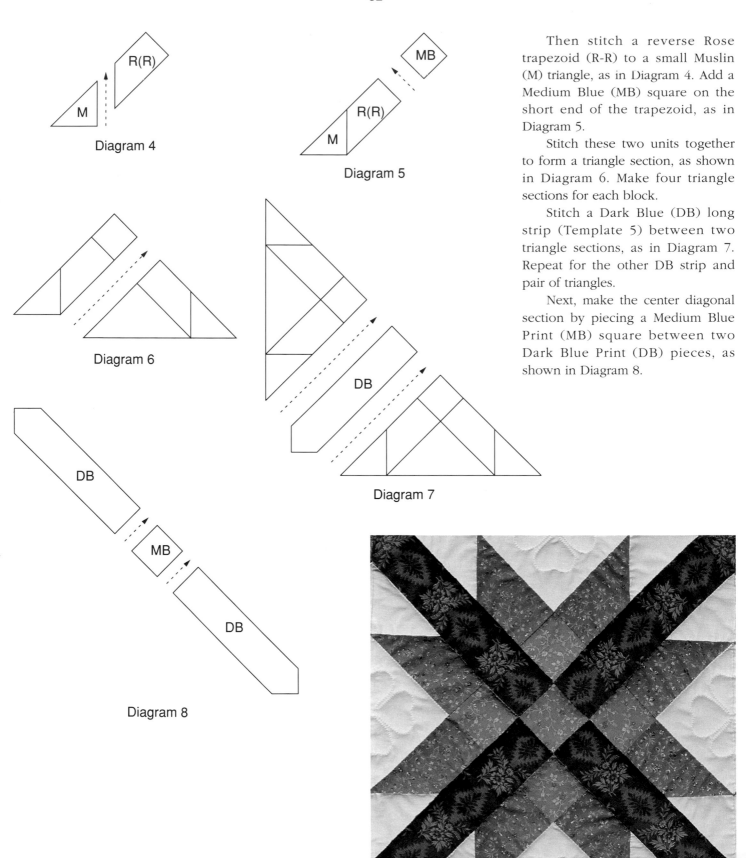

Diagram 4

Diagram 5

Diagram 6

Diagram 7

Diagram 8

Then stitch a reverse Rose trapezoid (R-R) to a small Muslin (M) triangle, as in Diagram 4. Add a Medium Blue (MB) square on the short end of the trapezoid, as in Diagram 5.

Stitch these two units together to form a triangle section, as shown in Diagram 6. Make four triangle sections for each block.

Stitch a Dark Blue (DB) long strip (Template 5) between two triangle sections, as in Diagram 7. Repeat for the other DB strip and pair of triangles.

Next, make the center diagonal section by piecing a Medium Blue Print (MB) square between two Dark Blue Print (DB) pieces, as shown in Diagram 8.

Complete the Mexican Star block by inserting this diagonal center strip between the large triangle sections, as in Diagram 9.

Make 20 blocks.

ASSEMBLY

Arrange the 20 blocks in five rows and four columns, as in Diagram 10. Piece the four blocks in Row 1 in short vertical seams, as shown in Diagram 11. Piece Rows 2 through 5 in a similar way. To complete the quilt center, join the five rows in long horizontal seams.

BORDERS

First, add the 4" Rose Print (R) borders. Miter the corners. Next, add the 3" Muslin (M) borders, followed by the outer 4" Navy Blue (N) borders. Miter all corners.

THE FINISHING TOUCH

QUILTING

From the 6 yards of muslin backing fabric, cut two three-yard lengths. Keep one intact (about 42" wide). From the other piece, cut two 21" widths. Join a 21" width to each side of the intact center panel. Press seams toward the outside.

Place the quilt backing right side down on a large, flat surface. Smooth the batting over it. Place the pressed quilt top over the batting, right side up. Pin or thread-baste the three layers together for quilting.

Use natural-color quilting thread to quilt "in-the-ditch" around the Mexican Star pieces, as suggested in

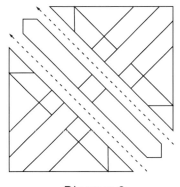

Diagram 9

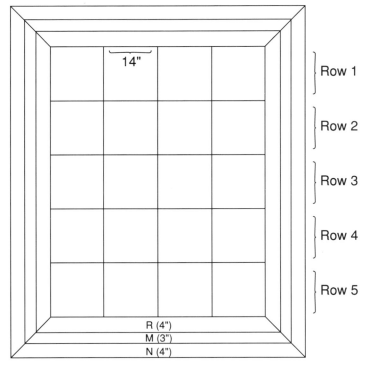

Diagram 10

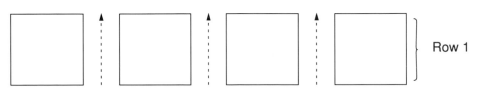

Diagram 11

Diagram 12. Use a washable marking pencil or soap chip to mark the four-leaf clover design in the large muslin squares. Mark three-leaf clover designs in the muslin border. Quilt the clover designs. Quilt parallel diagonal lines on the borders.

BINDING

Trim the batting to ½" larger than the quilt top, to allow for filler in the binding. Trim the backing to match the top. From the one yard of Navy Blue binding fabric, make 3" wide, continuous bias.

Fold the binding in half lengthwise, wrong sides together. Then attach it to the quilt front in a seam that penetrates all the layers. Turn the binding to the back and whipstitch it in place.

Diagram 12

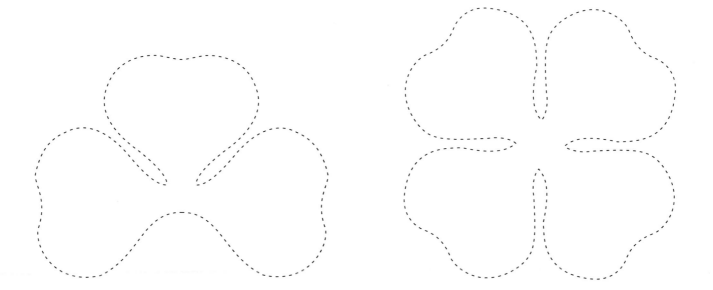

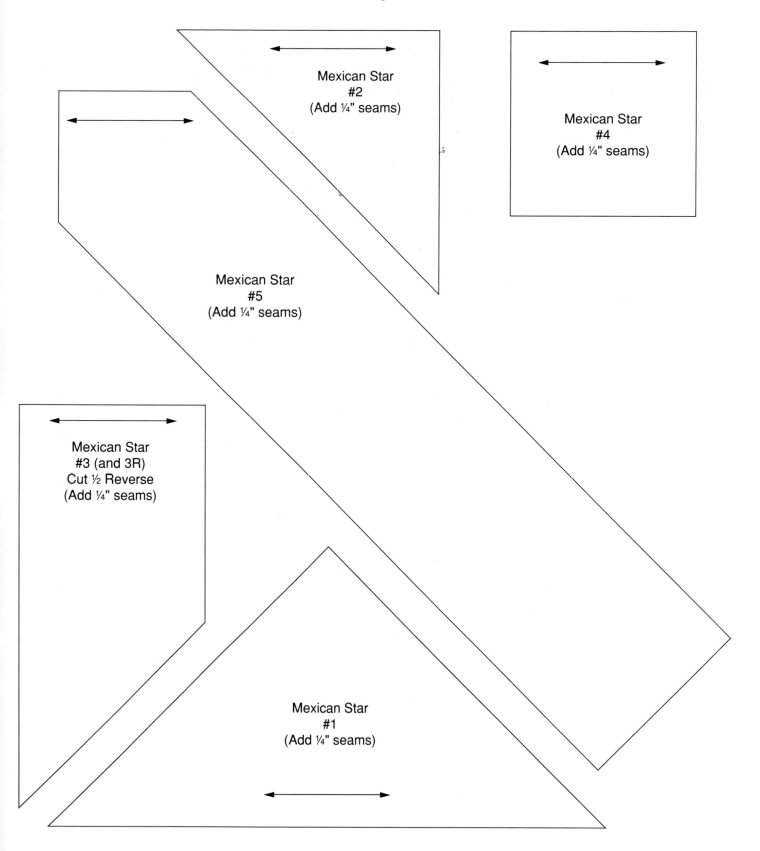

Mexican Star
#2
(Add ¼" seams)

Mexican Star
#4
(Add ¼" seams)

Mexican Star
#5
(Add ¼" seams)

Mexican Star
#3 (and 3R)
Cut ½ Reverse
(Add ¼" seams)

Mexican Star
#1
(Add ¼" seams)

LINKING THE PAST AND PRESENT
(TEXAS STARS)
Quilt by Jane Noll, Alma, Wisconsin

LINKING THE PAST AND PRESENT

Fibers and fabric have been an important part of Jane Noll's life. As an active mother and grandmother, farm woman, church leader and 4-H leader, Jane has been designing and constructing with needle, thread, and cloth for many years. It was a natural transition when she stepped into the world of quilts about ten years ago.

In addition to her needle art skills, Jane is an avid spokeswoman for historic preservation, especially at the community level, but also in a personal and family sense. Several of her quilts feature old blocks and pieces gleaned from family members – mothers, grandmothers, great-grandmothers, even great-great-grandmothers.

One of Jane's early projects was a large Ohio Rose appliqué quilt which had been started in a generation past. Jane gathered the unfinished blocks, completed the appliqué, added a complementary latticework, and assembled them into a lovely colorful quilt. Another box of Tumbling Block triangles made its way into a striking wall piece, which she presented to her daughter.

Texas Stars is another of Jane's efforts to link the generations of her family. The Eight-Point stars were pieced in 1908 by Kathryn Roback Rambath. Jane stitched a few remaining unfinished stars, to make 18 completed stars. To this she added the blue/gray background corners and squares. The completed blocks were set in a diagonal "on-point" arrangement. A contrasting rosy "sister" print was selected for the outer triangles.

Texas Stars was the pattern name used by Kathryn Rambath. It is familiar to quiltmakers as the classic Eight-Point star, known also as the LeMoyne Star, Blazing Star, or Lone Star. The mixture of fabrics – bold swirling florals, wide and narrow gingham checks, stripes, windowpanes, light shirting material, and fine prints, clearly marks this as a scrap project. In addition to the great variety of fabrics, some stars include more than just the two customary fabrics. At least eight of the 18 blocks include more than two scrap fabrics. The random fashion in which the pieces were cut from the cloth (some on grain, some off grain; some uniformly placed, others not) also confirms the "make-do" nature of the original project.

After completing the blocks, assembling the top, and hand quilting the piece, Jane presented it to her granddaughter, Carmen Noll. A label with the following inscription has been attached to the reverse side of the quilt:

To Carmen Jane Noll
Texas Stars made by Great-Great-Grandmother
Kathryn Roback Rambath in 1908
Hand-pieced and quilted by Grandmother
Jane Herold Noll in 1987

Texas Stars reaches across five generations, combining the old and the new. With needle, thread, and cloth, Jane has successfully linked the present to the past.

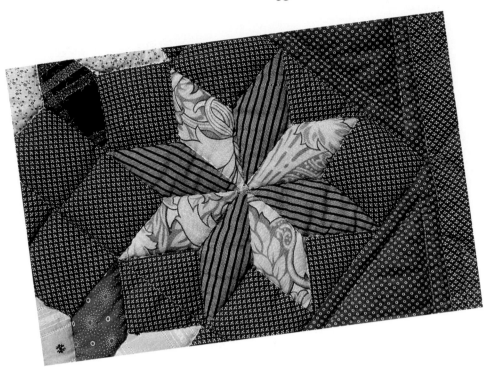

LINKING THE PAST AND PRESENT

FOR STARTERS

The following list will help you enjoy a smooth start and steady progress in your work on the Texas Stars quilt. It contains a variety of general information about making the quilt.

- Wash and press all fabrics before you begin.
- A variety of fabric scraps is suggested for the Eight-Point stars.
- Two print fabrics are needed for the star background, borders, and binding.
- All seams are ¼".
- For templates (patterns of the quilt pieces) use sturdy plastic, cardboard, or sandpaper, and be sure to note grain lines.
- Piecing may be done by hand or machine. For hand piecing, make the templates without seam allowances, and add them when marking and cutting the fabrics. For machine piecing, include the ¼" seam allowances on the templates.
- Eighteen pieced stars are required.
- Each pieced block measures 8" square, finished.
- Construction is by direct set of the blocks, with filler side and corner triangles.
- The dark blue border is 4" wide.
- The finished size for the Texas Stars quilt is 41" x 52".

SUPPLIES

Use 44"/45" wide cotton or cotton polyester blends.

Quilt Top:

Scraps: A variety of print fabrics, including stripes and checks, fairly evenly divided between darks and lights. A minimum of 36 fabrics allows for two different fabrics in each star. The minimum scrap size is a rectangle about 6" x 10". Stars may also be pieced from a complete random mixture of scraps. For new yardage, buy ⅛ yard each of 36 fabrics.

Dark Blue Print: 1¾ yards.

Rose Print: 2 yards (includes binding).

Binding: Included in Rose Print above.

Backing: 1¾ yards of good quality unbleached muslin.

Batting: Use a 45" x 60" (crib size) bonded polyester batt.

OTHER SUPPLIES

- Iron
- Material for templates
- Marking pencils or soap chips
- Scissors (for paper and fabric)
- Rulers
- Thread for piecing
- Pins
- Thread or safety pins for basting
- Quilting needles
- One spool natural-color quilting thread
- Thimble
- Long straightedge
- Hoop or frame for quilting

READY TO WORK

COLOR AND FABRIC KEY

D = Dark Scrap

L = Light Scrap

B = Blue Print (background and borders)

R = Rose Print
(side and corner triangles)

TEMPLATES

Begin by making templates of the five Texas Star pattern pieces (1, 2, 3, 4, and 5). Mark the grain line on each template. Note that ¼" seams must be added on all sides of each piece. Also note that Template 5 must be enlarged as directed.

CUTTING

Begin with the scrap fabrics. For each star, cut four Light (L) diamonds and four Dark (D) diamonds using Template 1. You will cut a total of 144 diamonds, and have a fairly even mix of lights and darks.

Continue with the Blue Print (B) fabric. Refer to Diagram 1 for a suggested cutting layout. Begin by cutting the four border pieces (allowances for seams and mitering included): Cut two side borders 4½" x 52½". Cut two end borders 4½" x 41½". Next, cut 72 squares from Template 2 and 72 triangles from Template 3. Be sure to adhere to the suggested grain lines indicated on the templates, in order to avoid any distortion of the pieced blocks.

Refer to Diagram 2 for a cutting layout for the Rose Print (R) fabric. Cut the following triangles, noting that Template 5 (side triangle) must be enlarged. Be sure to adhere to the suggested grain lines and add seams:

Cut four corner triangles from Template 4.

Cut ten side and end triangles from the enlarged Template 5.

Set aside the remaining Rose Print for binding.

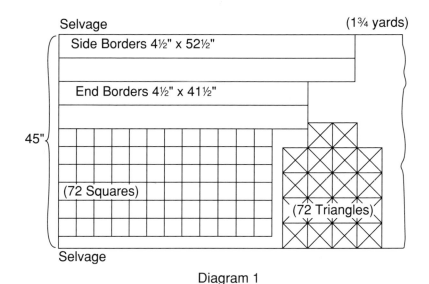

Diagram 1

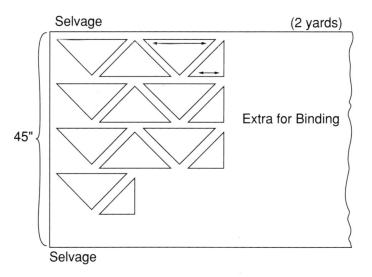

Diagram 2

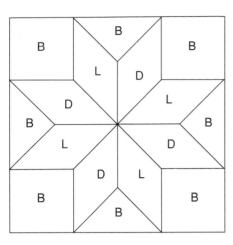

Diagram 3

PUTTING IT TOGETHER

BLOCK PIECING

Begin by collecting the 16 pieces that make up a star block (four dark diamonds, four light diamonds, four squares, and four triangles). Place the pieces right sides up on a flat surface, according to Diagram 3. Refer to Diagram 4 for the piecing order steps for each star. Complete the block by adding the corner squares and side triangles, as shown in Diagram 5. For hand piecing, this may be accomplished in continuous pivot seams, as suggested by the arrows. Continue arranging and piecing stars until you have 18 completed 8" stars.

ASSEMBLY

Refer to Diagram 6 for the general layout of the Texas Stars quilt. Place the 18 blocks on a large, flat surface, each set "on point" in a diagonal arrangement. Number each block with a small label, numbers 1 through 18, according to Diagram 6.

Next, place the ten side and end triangles and four corner triangles to fill in the background.

The blocks are assembled in a diagonal fashion, in six panels, as suggested in Diagram 7. Begin with the upper-left corner of the quilt. Piece two large Rose Print (R) triangles around Block 1, as shown in Diagram 8. Add a corner triangle to complete the unit.

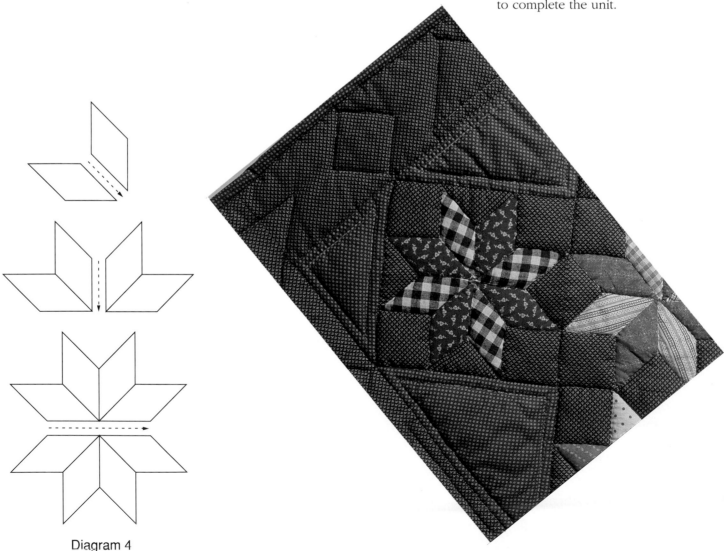

Diagram 4

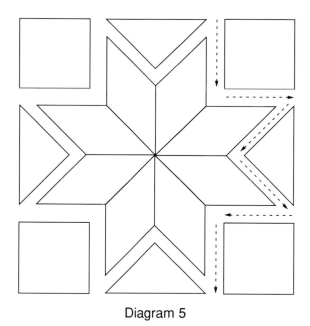

Diagram 5

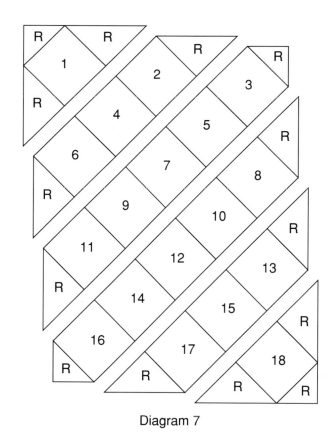

Diagram 7

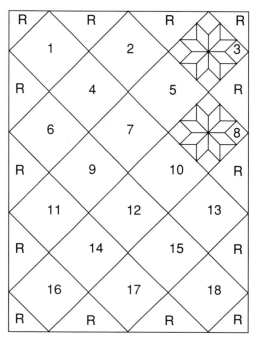

Diagram 6

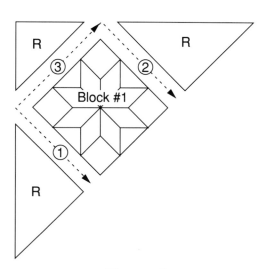

Diagram 8

Make a similar unit with Block 18 for the lower-right corner of the quilt.

Next, make a diagonal section with Blocks 2, 4, and 6. Attach a large triangle on each end, as shown in Diagram 9. Make a similar section with Blocks 13, 15, and 17.

Complete a middle section by joining Blocks 3, 5, 7, 9, and 11. Add a large side triangle to Block 11 and a small corner triangle on the opposite end, on Block 3, as shown in Diagram 10. Make a similar diagonal section with Blocks 8, 10, 12, 14, and 16.

Stitch the six diagonal sections together to complete the Texas Stars quilt top.

BORDERS

Add the 4" Dark Blue borders to complete the quilt top.

THE FINISHING TOUCH

QUILTING

Place the washed and pressed 1¾ yard muslin backing fabric right side down on a large, flat surface. Smooth the batting over it. Place the pressed quilt top over the batting, right side up. Pin or thread-baste the three layers together for quilting.

Use natural-color quilting thread to quilt "in-the-ditch" (close to the seam) around each piece in the stars, as suggested in Diagram 11. Outline stitch about ¼" from the edges of each side, end, and corner triangle.

Make stencils from the suggested square and triangle quilt designs. Mark and quilt alternate squares and triangles in the blue border. Place a triangle in each corner. Add three squares (set "on point") and two triangles on each end. Add four squares and three triangles on each side, as suggested in Diagram 11.

BINDING

Trim the batting to ½" larger than the quilt top, to allow for filler in the binding. Trim the backing to match the top. From the remaining Rose Print (R) fabric, make 3" wide continuous bias binding.

Fold the binding in half lengthwise, wrong sides together. Then attach it to the quilt front in a seam that penetrates all the layers. Turn the binding to the back and whipstitch it in place.

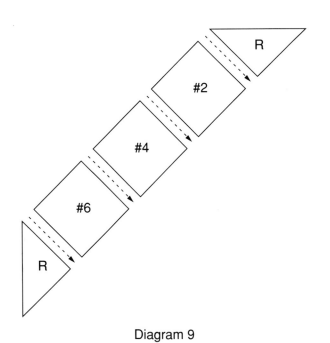

Diagram 9

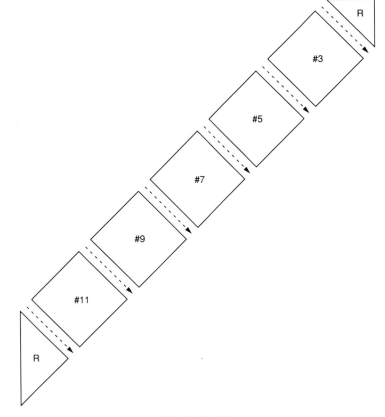

Diagram 10

Diagram 11

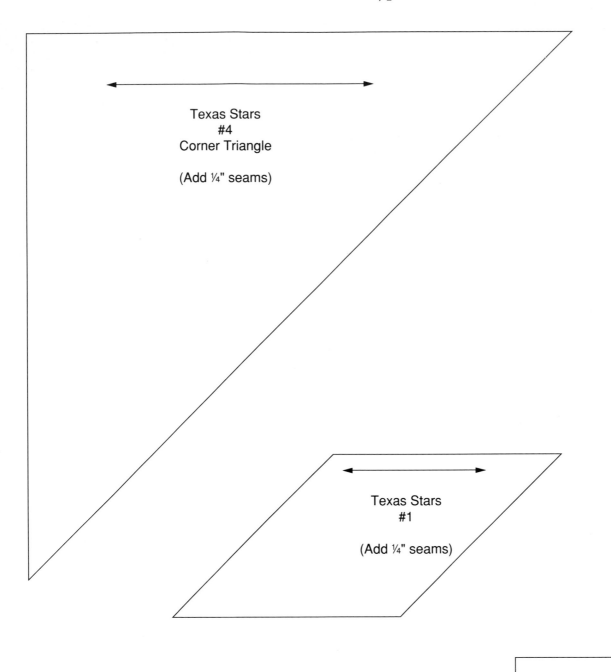

Texas Stars
#4
Corner Triangle

(Add ¼" seams)

Texas Stars
#1

(Add ¼" seams)

Texas Stars
#2

(Add ¼" seams)

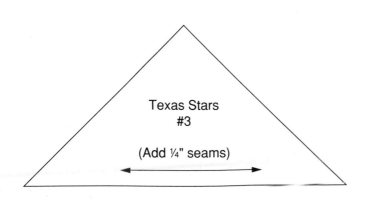

Texas Stars
#3

(Add ¼" seams)

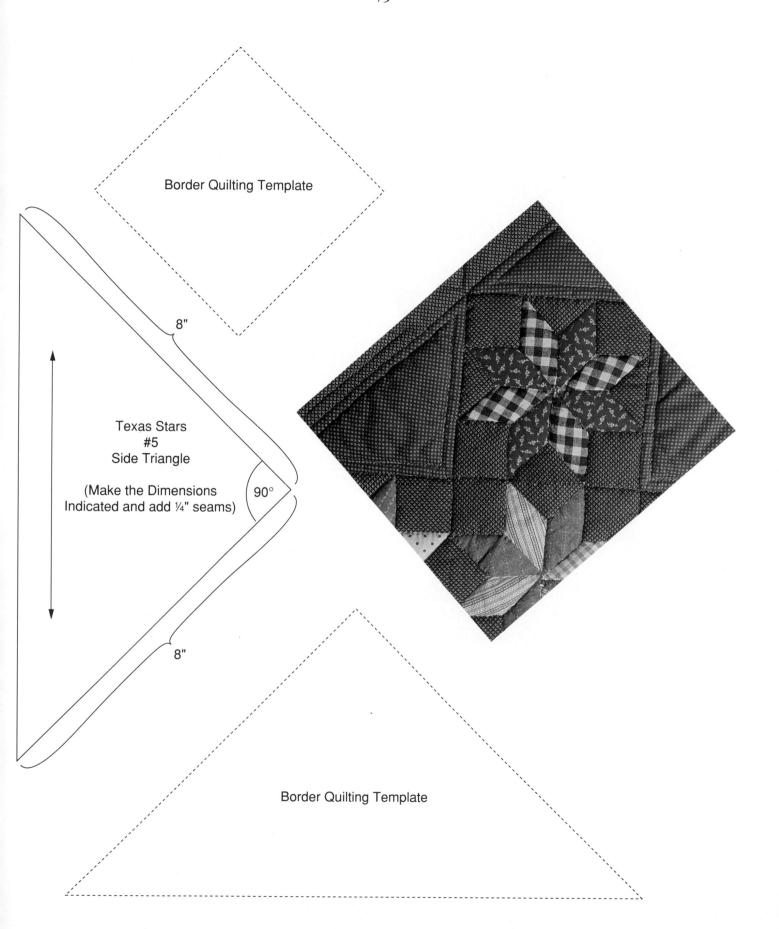

Border Quilting Template

8"

Texas Stars
#5
Side Triangle

(Make the Dimensions
Indicated and add ¼" seams)

90°

8"

Border Quilting Template

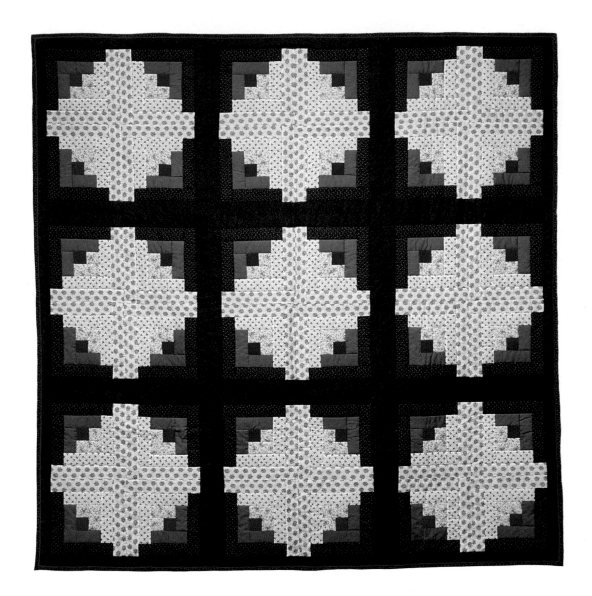

GRAPHIC BEAUTY
(LOG CABIN)
Quilt by Mary Mousel, Eau Claire, Wisconsin

GRAPHIC BEAUTY

The Log Cabin has already taken its well-earned place beside other long-admired quilts like the Lone Star, Rose of Sharon, and Double Wedding Ring. One of the most popular quilt patterns of all time, Log Cabin is often the first block attempted by quiltmakers.

The history of the Log Cabin extends back more than a century. Yet numerous variations continue to be assembled. Several modern methods of streamlined construction have been developed. Early traditional techniques used backing fabrics to which individually cut pieces were carefully sewn. Contemporary shortcuts emphasize anything from cut and chop centers to one-step piecing and quilting. Some quiltmakers suggest using a paper cutter (an 18" office paper cutter), slicing through fabrics in one clean sweep. Others wield the rotary cutter from bolt to bolt, then stitch and cut strips and rotate blocks in assembly-line fashion.

The basic Log Cabin block with its strong light/dark diagonal division is a masterpiece of design. Its elements are simple – a square and rectangles (or logs). Traditional sets include the familiar Barn Raising, Straight Furrow, Streak of Lightning, and Light and Dark. Blocks have been altered and rotated into Pinwheels, Birds-in-Flight, Courthouse Steps, and Pineapple. Central medallion styles have been popular, and Log Cabin blocks have been effectively combined with other traditional blocks such as Stars and Virginia Reels.

Log Cabin designers have set the block on point with suggestions of an "L" formation, or "W's," and "V's." The block has also been adapted into other shapes like hexagons, triangles, diamonds, and parallelograms. Some designers have explored the optical illusion of creating curves from perfectly straight pieces by setting the Log Cabin "off-center." As one of my quilting friends noted, "It's nice. With Log Cabin you can get real technical with a simple thing."

Mary Mousel selected a very graphic setting for her Log Cabin. Her use of neutrals in a broad range of light to dark, from white to deep charcoal gray, is accented with bright scarlet centers. This red square becomes the accent, the focal point of each block, and is further enhanced by narrow red piping in the border.

Mary used a one-step construction method. All piecing and quilting is done by machine in this method, which was popularized in women's magazines in the late 1970's. The steps for this "all-in-one" technique are illustrated in the pattern directions. For someone who has never pieced a Log Cabin block, the prospect may at first seem intimidating. But once you get the hang of it (I suggest a practice block), you will find it an easy and relaxing process.

Mary's Log Cabin is one in a large stack of beautiful quilts that she has made. Since she began sewing over 60 years ago, quiltmaking has come and gone and come back again to a scene that included dressmaking, tailoring, drapery making, and professional gardening. One of her innovative fabric mixture quilts, a Round the Twist variation, is featured in the book, *Award-Winning Scrap Quilts.*

In addition to guild and museum showings, Mary's Log Cabin has hung in businesses and galleries. It didn't take long for a discerning quilt enthusiast to recognize its graphic beauty. It is now in a private collection.

LOG CABIN

FOR STARTERS

The following list will help you enjoy a smooth start and steady progress in your work on the Log Cabin quilt.

It contains a variety of general information about making the quilt:

- Wash and press all fabrics before you begin.
- A minimum of seven fabrics is required – three lights, three darks, and a red center. A mixture of scrap fabrics is a good alternative for the Log Cabin quilt.
- All seams are ¼".
- Seven pattern pieces are required.
- For templates (patterns of the quilt pieces) use sturdy plastic, cardboard, or sandpaper, and be sure to note grain lines.
- Piecing and quilting are done by machine using a quick method of stitching through all three layers of the quilt.
- Each pieced block measures 14" square, finished.
- An optional red piping and a dark binding frame the quilt.
- The finished size for the Log Cabin quilt is 84" square.

- A Log Cabin worksheet for sketching light/dark and color options is included in the Appendix.

SUPPLIES

Use 44"/45" cotton or cotton polyester blends.

Quilt Top:

Light Prints (gray or black fine prints on a white background):
  Light 1: ¾ yard
  Light 2: 1¾ yards
  Light 3: 2¼ yards
Dark Prints (solid gray, white print on black, or deep charcoal):
  Dark 1: 1¼ yards
  Dark 2: 2 yards
  Dark 3: 2¾ yards
Red (for centers): ¼ yard
NOTE: Increase the red amount to one yard if you plan to include the optional red piping in the outer border.

Binding: Buy an additional one yard of the second dark fabric OR a deep charcoal gray solid.

Backing: 8½ yards of good quality unbleached muslin

Batting: Two 72" x 90" (twin-size)

bonded polyester batts.

OTHER SUPPLIES

- Iron
- Material for templates
- Marking pencils or soap chips
- Scissors (for paper and fabric)
- Rulers
- Two or more spools of thread for machine piecing (in a neutral color to blend with fabrics)
- Pins
- Long straightedge
- 10 yards of cord for piping (optional)

READY TO WORK

COLOR AND FABRIC KEY
L = Light (1, 2, and 3)
D = Dark (1, 2, and 3)
R = Red
TEMPLATES

Begin by making templates of all seven Log Cabin pattern pieces (A, B, C, D, E, F, and G). Note that patterns E, F, and G must be enlarged to the appropriate size. Note that ¼" seams must be added on all sides of each piece. Mark the grain lines on each template.

CUTTING

Begin with the Light Print fabrics. Cut the following pieces. Be sure to adhere to the suggested grain lines.

Light 1 – Cut 36 of Template A
Cut 36 of Template B
Light 2 – Cut 36 of Template C
Cut 36 of Template D
Light 3 – Cut 36 of Template E
Cut 36 of Template F

Continue with the Dark Print fabrics. Cut the following pieces:

Dark 1 – Cut 36 of Template B
Cut 36 of Template C
Dark 2 – Cut 36 of Template D
Cut 36 of Template E
Dark 3 – Cut 36 of Template F
Cut 36 of Template G

From the 8½ yards of muslin backing fabric, cut 36 squares, each 16" x 16".

Next, cut 36 pieces of batting, each 16" x 16".

PUTTING IT TOGETHER

BLOCK PIECING

Refer to the illustration in Diagram 1 and note that the Log Cabin block is divided diagonally into half light and half dark fabrics around the red center.

Collect the 15 pieces needed to complete one block (one red center, seven light and seven dark). Place the pieces right sides up on a flat surface in the order shown in Diagrams 1 and 2.

Begin by pinning a square of batting onto the wrong side of a muslin backing square, as in Diagram 3. The batting and backing blocks have been cut somewhat larger than necessary, so there will be an excess of batting and backing around the pieced blocks.

Pin a red square in the exact middle of the batting (measure from all four edges to be sure), as in Diagram 4. Next, place a square of the first Light (L1) right side down on the center red square. Pin and stitch in a ¼" seam through all four layers (light print, red center, batting, backing), as shown in Diagram 5. Open out the light print fabric and finger press.

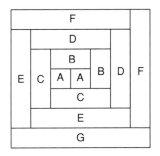

Diagram 1

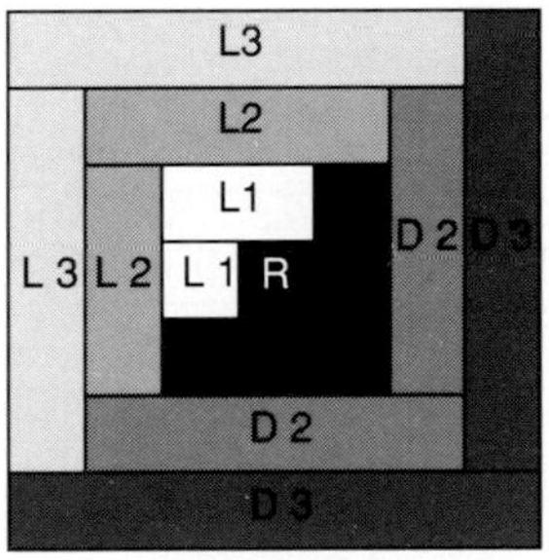

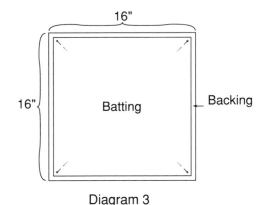

Diagram 2

Diagram 3

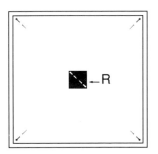

Diagram 4

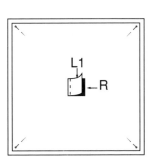

Diagram 5

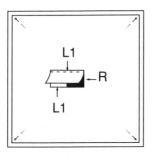

Diagram 6

Continue by adding the other Light 1 piece (B, 2" x 4") in a seam through all layers, as in Diagram 6. Open out, finger press, and continue by adding the next piece, which is Dark 1 (also template B), as in Diagram 7.

Continue adding pieces in a clockwise fashion, using Diagrams 1 and 2 as your guide.

Make 36 pieced blocks.

JOINING BLOCKS

Arrange the blocks in the Light/Dark groupings suggested by the photograph and Diagram 8. This is accomplished by grouping the light sides of four blocks together to form a light "diamond" shape.

Place six blocks across and six blocks down, as in Diagram 9. Assemble the blocks in horizontal rows by placing two pieced blocks right sides together. Pin the pieced block edges together, as in Diagram 10. Stitch together, holding the batting and backing free from the seam. Add the remaining blocks to complete a row (total of six blocks).

Make five more rows.

To finish the seams on the back, trim the batting pieces so the edges of the batting are flush. Then trim and fold the seam allowance on one backing piece over the adjacent backing piece, as in Diagram 11. Blindstitch through the backing

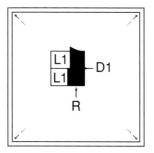

Diagram 7

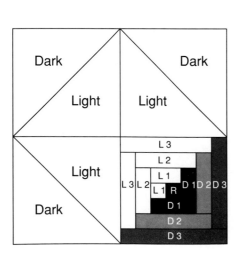

Diagram 8

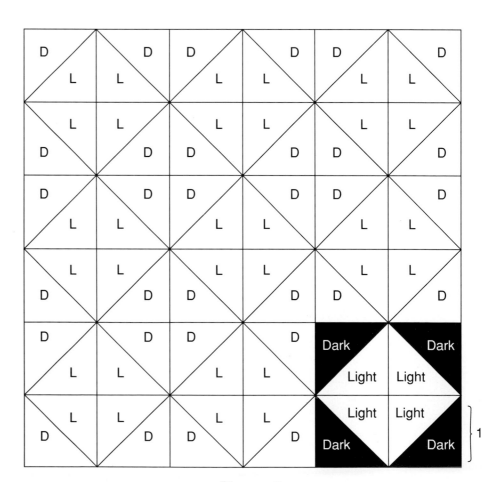

Diagram 9

material being careful that the stitches do not carry through to the quilt front.

Stitch the six panels in long horizontal seams, keeping the batting and backing fabric free as before. Then finish off the back by turning and blindstitching as before.

THE FINISHING TOUCH

BINDING

Trim the batting to ½" larger than the quilt top, to allow for filler in the binding. Trim the backing to match the top. For the piping (optional), use the remaining red fabric and piping cord. Pin and baste the piping to the edge of the quilt with the raw edges to the outside.

From the remaining dark fabric (2) or deep charcoal gray binding fabric, make 3" wide continuous bias binding.

Fold the binding in half lengthwise, wrong sides together. Then attach it to the quilt front in a seam that penetrates all the layers. Turn the binding to the back and whipstitch it in place.

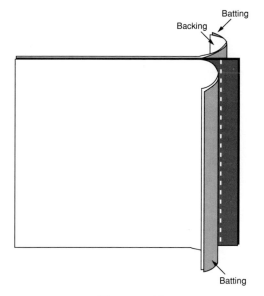

Diagram 10

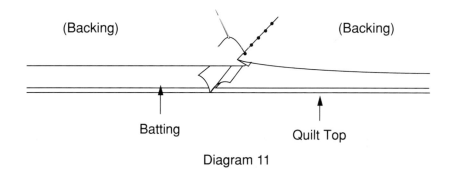

Diagram 11

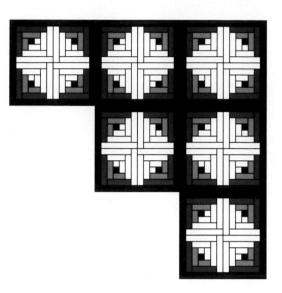

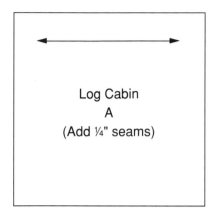

Log Cabin
A
(Add ¼" seams)

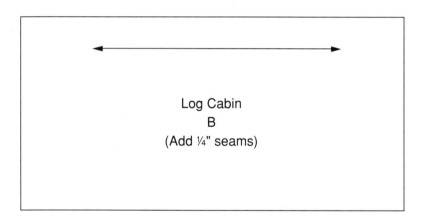

Log Cabin
B
(Add ¼" seams)

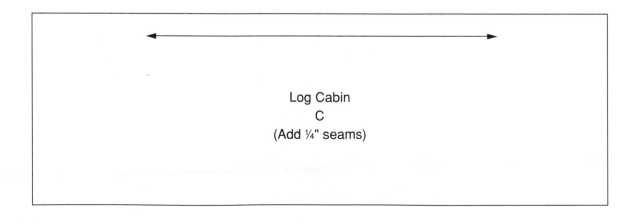

Log Cabin
C
(Add ¼" seams)

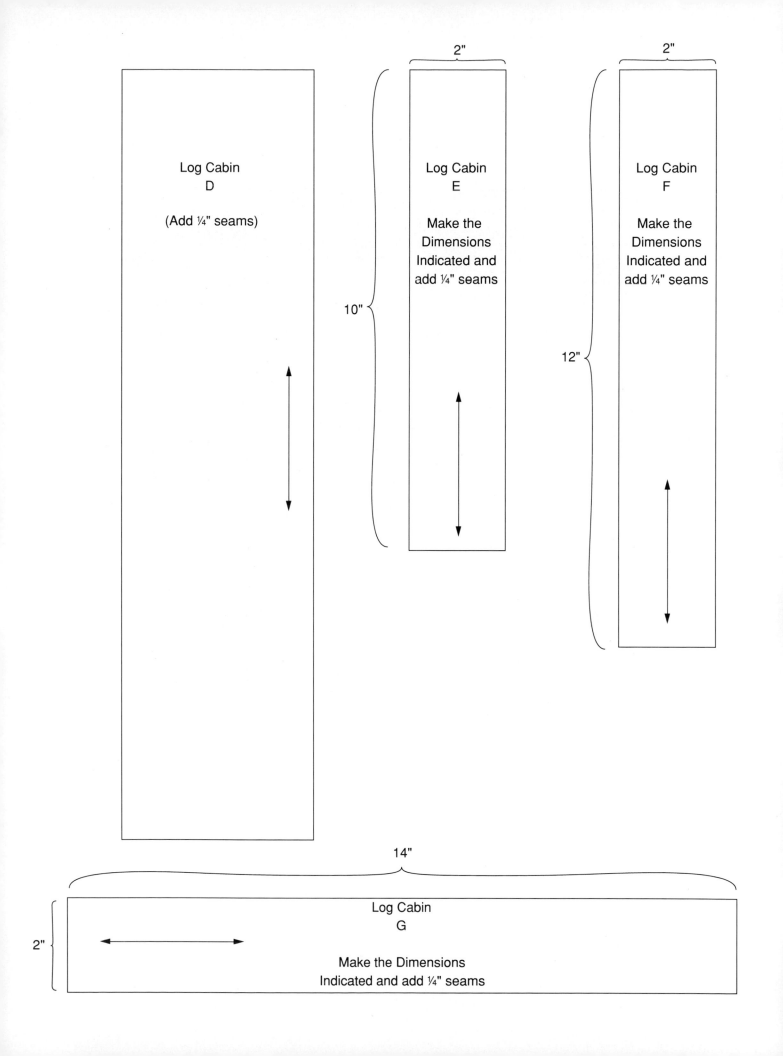

Log Cabin
D

(Add ¼" seams)

2"

Log Cabin
E

Make the
Dimensions
Indicated and
add ¼" seams

10"

2"

Log Cabin
F

Make the
Dimensions
Indicated and
add ¼" seams

12"

14"

Log Cabin
G

Make the Dimensions
Indicated and add ¼" seams

2"

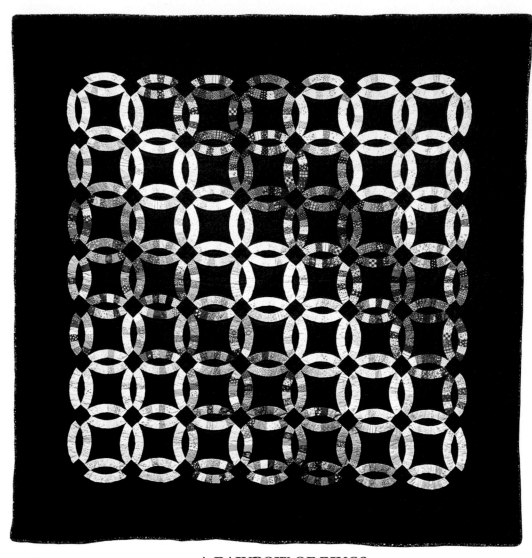

A RAINBOW OF RINGS
(DOUBLE WEDDING RING)
Quilt by Gladys Hayes, Altoona, Wisconsin

A RAINBOW OF RINGS

A rainbow array of colors against a field of black is about as breathtaking an effect as can be accomplished in fabric. Amish quilters have been doing it successfully for generations. Other quiltmakers have been slower to realize the dramatic beauty of multicolored fabrics against a deep dark background.

When Gladys Hayes began planning her Double Wedding Ring quilt, black was not one of the colors foremost in her mind. She was designing a quilt for her teenage granddaughter, Alicia Pose. Gladys shared several quilt books, patterns, pictures, and ideas with Alicia. The classic Double Wedding Ring, with colorful mixed fabrics against a black background captured her attention. Her preference for a rich mixture of colors, from delicate pastels to somber black, was clear.

Gladys' Double Wedding Ring includes more than 150 fabrics, some from her scrap bag, others purchased in shops along the way as she accompanied her husband to seminars and conferences in several states. Each fabric was cut into tiny segments (by tiny, I mean some of the pieces are only about an inch square, some smaller). Segments were hand pieced into strips, strips into ovals, ovals into rings.

The rings were arranged in a rainbow format set diagonally from one corner of the quilt to the other. Beginning with yellow in the upper right corner, rings progress into golds and oranges, reds and pinks, lavenders, blues, and greens, and back to yellow. Gladys has skillfully pieced and positioned her fabrics for subtle color transition, moving through intense vivid hues and delicate mellow colors. The impression of diagonal panels of colored light is very effective.

The variety of fabrics that Gladys collected, the sheer number of pieces she cut, and the many hours of piecing and quilting attest not only to Gladys' needlework skill and patience, but also her dedication to her granddaughter. Gladys presented this lovely quilt to Alicia on her 16th birthday.

DOUBLE WEDDING RING

FOR STARTERS

The following list will help you enjoy a smooth start and steady progress in your work on the Double Wedding Ring quilt. It contains a variety of general information about making the quilt:

- Wash and press all fabrics before you begin.
- A large colorful variety of light and medium scraps is a good choice for the Double Wedding Ring.
- All seams are ¼".
- The "rings" are assembled and arranged in a rainbow color format – yellow, green, blue, lavender, red, and orange/rust.
- The five pieces of the Double Wedding Ring quilt require curved piecing techniques, so some previous piecing experience is recommended.
- For templates (patterns of the quilt pieces) use sturdy plastic, cardboard, or sandpaper, and be sure to note grain lines.
- Piecing may be done by hand or machine. For hand piecing, make the templates without seam allowances, and add them when marking and cutting the fabrics. For machine piecing, include the ¼" seam allowances on the templates.
- The top is composed of 49 interlocking rings.
- All background areas, corner squares, and borders are black.
- The finished size for the Double Wedding Ring quilt is 73" square.

SUPPLIES

Use 44"/45" wide cotton or cotton polyester blends.

Quilt Top:

Light and Medium Print Fabrics or Scraps: At least eight different fabrics are needed. A larger variety of scraps is recommended (dozens or even hundreds; the broader the variety and color range, the better).

Black: 6½ yards

Binding: 1 yard of a dark print (such as small colored flowers against black).

Backing: 4½ yards of good quality unbleached muslin.

Batting: Use an 81" x 96" (double size) bonded polyester batt.

OTHER SUPPLIES

- Iron
- Material for templates
- Marking pencils (including a light one) or soap chips
- Scissors (for paper and fabric)
- Rulers
- Thread for piecing and appliqué
- Pins
- Thread or safety pins for basting
- Quilting needles
- Two spools black quilting thread
- Thimble
- Hoop or frame for quilting

READY TO WORK

COLOR AND FABRIC KEY

S = Scrap

B = Black

R = Reverse Template

TEMPLATES

Begin by making templates of all five of the Double Wedding Ring pattern pieces (1 through 5). Mark the grain lines on each template. Note that ¼" seams must be added on all sides of each piece. Also note the center side markings on Templates 4 and 5.

CUTTING

Begin with the Scrap (S) fabrics.

Use a wide variety of colors and styles to cut the following number of pieces:

Template 1: Cut 896.

Template 2: Cut 448. (Half of these must be cut with the reverse template.)

From the Black (B) fabric, first cut four border pieces 11" (or as wide as the fabric width divided into fourths will allow) by 75" (allowances for seams and mitering included).

Next, cut the following background and corner pieces from the Black (B) fabric:

Template 3 (small square): Cut 224.

Template 4 (oval): Cut 112.

Template 5 (center of ring): Cut 49.

PUTTING IT TOGETHER

DESIGN DECISIONS

The overall color arrangement of your Double Wedding Ring quilt should be made now. If you choose to work in a rainbow array similar to the pictured quilt, you will need to group your scrap pieces by color and make each oval unit with a predominant color.

As you proceed with the piecing of oval units, it will be helpful to consider where they will be placed on the quilt. After you have completed all the oval units (112), arrange them on a large, flat surface and then plan the assembly of your quilt top.

PIECING

Refer to Diagram 1 for placement of the pieces in the Double Wedding Ring oval unit. Collect the pieces necessary for one oval (12 scrap pieces, two black squares, and one black oval piece). Lay the pieces right side up on a flat surface, according to the diagram. Note the placement of the two reverse (R) pieces.

To make the arc as shown in Diagram 2, stitch four #1 scrap pieces together. Then piece a #2 and a reverse #2R to each end. Press seams to one side.

Next, add a Black (B) oval, as shown in Diagram 3, being careful to match the center marking with the middle of the pieced arc. Press the seam toward the oval.

For the other portion of the oval, make an arc as described above (six pieces shown in Diagram 2). Then add a Black (B) square on each end, as shown in Diagram 4.

Attach this elongated arc to the previously pieced unit, as shown in Diagram 5. This completes the oval unit. Make 112 oval units.

ASSEMBLY

Lay all your ovals and large black centers on a flat surface. Arrange the colors according to your plan or preference. Refer to Diagram 6 for a piecing layout of the quilt top, which is composed of seven rows. Each row contains different units (I and II, as shown in Diagram 7) or black centers (5).

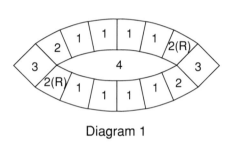

Diagram 1

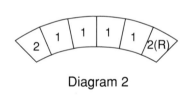

Diagram 2

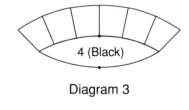

Diagram 3

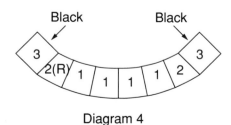

Diagram 4

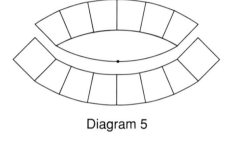

Diagram 5

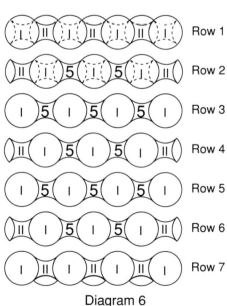

Row 1
Row 2
Row 3
Row 4
Row 5
Row 6
Row 7

Diagram 6

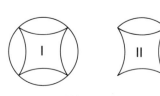

Diagram 7

Begin with the top row (Row 1) which is made up of four complete rings (Unit I) and three partial rings (Unit II), as shown in Diagram 8.

To make a complete ring (Unit I), piece an oval to the large center Black (B) piece (Template #5), as shown in Diagram 9. Pin and match the center markings. Stitch the seam and press it toward the oval.

Add another oval to the opposite side of the black center piece, as shown in Diagram 10. Then add an oval to each side, to complete the ring, as shown in Diagram 11.

To make a Unit II, add one oval to the center black piece, as shown in Diagram 12.

To complete Row 1, stitch the four complete rings (Unit I) and three of Unit II, referring back to Diagram 8.

Proceed with Row 2, which is composed of three complete rings (Unit I), two of Unit II, and two Black (B) centers, as shown in Diagram 13.

Continue with the remaining five rows, using Diagram 6 as a guide. Then join the seven rows in long cross seams to complete the pieced top.

BORDERS

Turn under ¼" on all of the outside edges of the pieced top. Press the turned edges. Center the pieced top over a black border piece, as in Diagram 14. Pin in place. Then appliqué the edge of the pieced top to the border with tiny stitches. Use thread to match the scrap fabrics. Begin and end the appliqué stitches at the dot markings.

Appliqué the opposite side of the quilt to another border panel.

Next, add the two remaining borders. Pin the pressed quilt edge over the borders and miter the corners of the border over the previously attached borders, as suggested by the broken lines in Diagram 14. Appliqué in place to complete the quilt top. Trim the excess border fabric from behind the mitered corners.

THE FINISHING TOUCH

QUILTING

From the 4½ yards of backing fabric, cut two 2¼ yard lengths. Keep one intact (about 42" wide). From the other piece, cut two 21" widths. Join a 21" width to each side of the intact center panel. Press the seams toward the outside.

Place the quilt backing right side down on a large, flat surface. Smooth the batting over it. Place the pressed quilt top over the batting, right side up. Pin or thread-baste the three layers together for quilting.

Use black quilting thread to outline quilt on each black center and each black oval, about ¼" from the edge, as suggested in Diagram

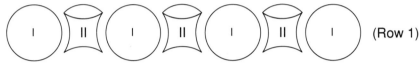

(Row 1)

Diagram 8

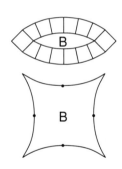

Diagram 9

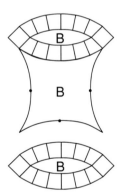

Diagram 10

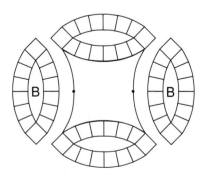

Diagram 11

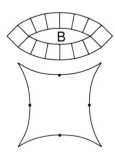

Diagram 12

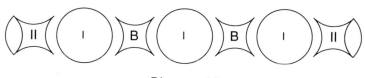

Diagram 13

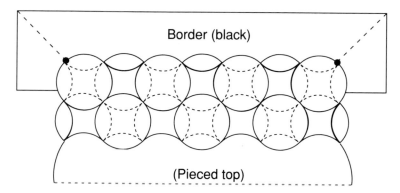

Border (black)

(Pieced top)

Diagram 14

15. Also, quilt ¼" from the outer edges of the outside rings.

Use a washable light-colored marking pencil or soap chip to mark the suggested cable pattern on the black borders. Quilt with black thread.

BINDING

Trim the batting to ½" larger than the quilt top, to allow for filler in the binding. Trim the backing to match the top. From the one yard of dark print fabric, make 3" wide continuous bias binding.

Fold the binding in half lengthwise, wrong sides together. Then attach it to the quilt front in a seam that penetrates all the layers. Turn the binding to the back and whipstitch it in place.

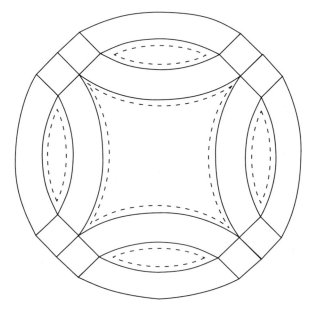

Diagram 15

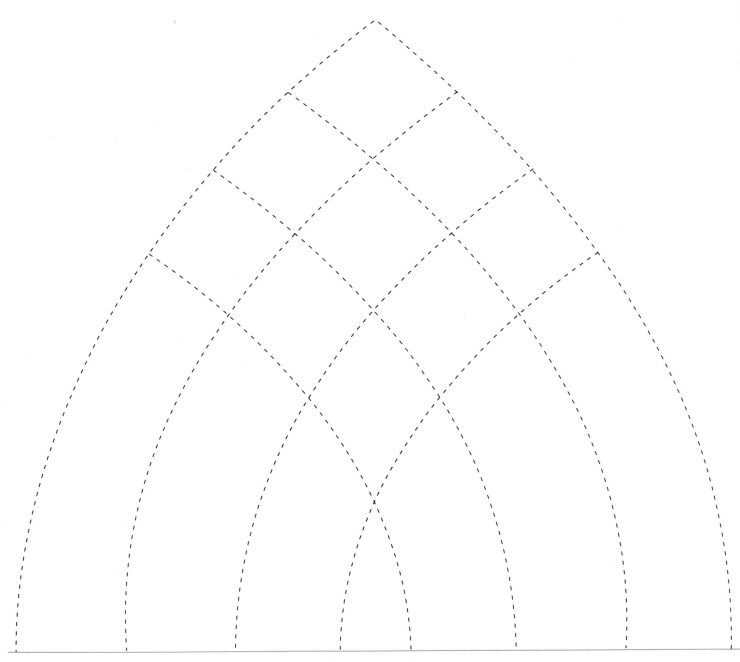

Cable Quilting Design (½ shown)

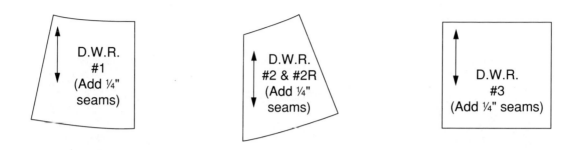

D.W.R.
#1
(Add ¼"
seams)

D.W.R.
#2 & #2R
(Add ¼"
seams)

D.W.R.
#3
(Add ¼" seams)

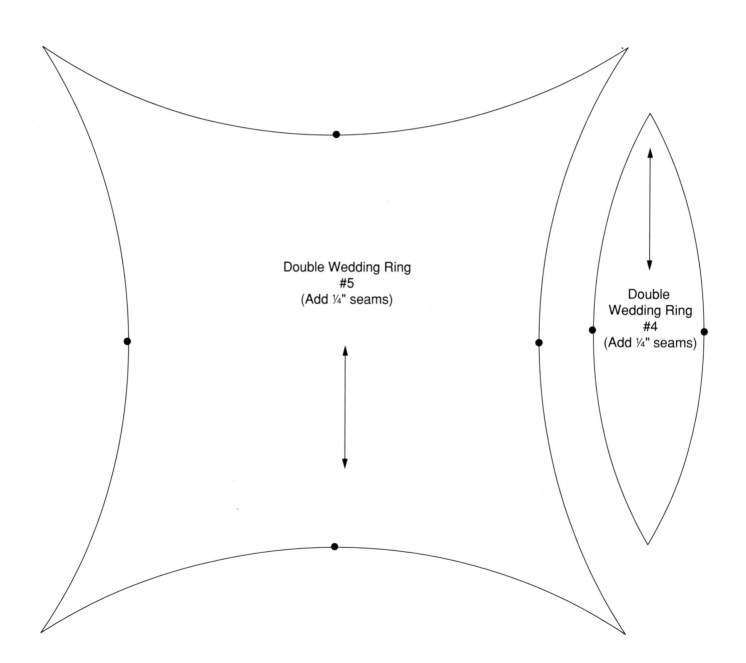

Double Wedding Ring
#5
(Add ¼" seams)

Double
Wedding Ring
#4
(Add ¼" seams)

THE FORMULA WORKS: SP + MR + EP = SGQ
(SPOOLS)
Quilt by the Clearwater Quilters, Eau Claire, Wisconsin

THE FORMULA WORKS: SP + MR + EP = SGQ

The Clearwater Quilters have yet to run out of ideas for their guild's charitable projects. Members have generously donated time, supplies, blocks, and quilts for a variety of worthy causes such as the women's refuge center and the pediatrics units of two local hospitals. The Spools quilt is another from their list of volunteer projects for community benefit. It was made and donated to the locally televised Easter Seal telethon auction. Spools is one of the cheeriest, upbeat group projects I have seen. Here is additional evidence that the formula for a successful group quilt project (SP + MR + EP = SGQ) works: Simple Pattern + Minimal Restrictions + Enthusiastic Participants = Successful Group Quilt.

Simple Pattern? Yes. Only two templates are required, a square and a trapezoid; only five pieces per Spool, 20 pieces for a finished block of four spools.

Minimal Restrictions? Yes. A striped or directional fabric was suggested for the square template. Add any light and dark for the trapezoids.

Enthusiastic Participants? Yes. More than 20 guild members cut, pieced, basted, quilted, bound, or contributed fabric for the Spools project.

Participants chose freely from the colors in their scrap collections. A rainbow of solids, fine prints, and directionals were used – pale yellows and golds, bright pinks and pale peaches, deep greens and browns, soft blues and lavenders.

Even the directional fabrics vary greatly. Some are very prominent, with two or three stripes in each piece, others subdued with numerous fine lines. Some are woven stripes, some printed; some very subtle with low contrast to the background fabric, others with highly visible sharp contrasting lines. One participant included plaid fabrics. All give an illusion of thread or yarn wound on the spool.

In the past few years, the Spools pattern has experienced renewed popularity. The traditional Spool design appeared in Ruby McKim's 1934 *One Hundred and One Patchwork Patterns*. It has since appeared in numerous other pattern books, periodicals, and calendars. Modern quilters have devised methods to enhance the design and streamline the piecing. Some variations include strip-piecing of narrow ribbons of fabric in the square template, resulting in an even stronger impression of filament wound on the spool.

Another technique suggests elimination of the inset (pivot) seams by cutting the center square into four small triangles. Although this may be attractive for machine piecing (some machine-piecers may feel handicapped by pivot seams), the cutting of the center square into four triangles may destroy the natural lines and shape of the design. The chopped up lines could be distracting, especially if stripes or plaids are used.

The Clearwater Quilters opted to emphasize the spools shape. However, other variations may be considered. Fabrics can be placed in a light/medium/dark arrangement to reveal a three-dimensional Maltese Cross as shown in Diagram A (page 99). Spools set end to end with the dark trapezoids adjacent form a six-sided figure reminiscent of Japanese Lanterns, as shown in Diagram B (page 99). Four hexagonal units around a square make a large octagon with curved illusion potential, as shown in Diagram C, also on page 99. A little exploration with your colored pencils and the spools worksheet will reveal still other options.

From the 35 carefully placed directionals to the colorful binding pieced from leftover fabrics, "Spools" is a handsome quilt. Thanks to the Clearwater Quilters for their generous donation. Thanks, too, for proof that the formula works.

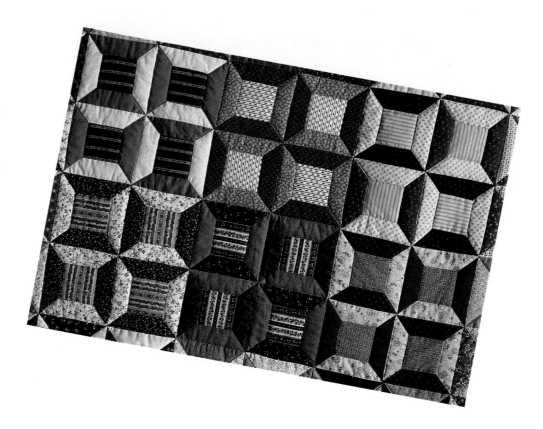

SPOOLS

FOR STARTERS

The following list will help you enjoy a smooth start and steady progress in your work on the Spools quilt. It contains a variety of general information about making the quilt:

- Wash and press all fabrics before you begin.
- A minimum of three fabrics is required – a light, a dark, and a print for each block.
- A variety of scraps, including plaids and stripes, will make a colorful fabric design.
- All seams are ¼".
- For templates (patterns of the quilt pieces) use sturdy plastic, cardboard, or sandpaper, and be sure to note grain lines.
- Piecing may be done by hand or machine. For hand piecing, make the templates without seam allowances, and add them when marking and cutting the fabrics. For machine piecing, include the ¼" seam allowances on the templates.

- The small spools measure 6" square; the blocks are 12" square, finished.
- Thirty-five pieced blocks are required.
- Three borders in dark green and beige surround the spools.
- The binding is pieced from the remaining scrap fabrics.
- The finished size for the Spools quilt is 78" x 102".

SUPPLIES

Use 44"/45" cotton or cotton polyester blends.

(Note that the fabrics in the photographed quilt will not correspond entirely with the following fabric suggestions. The quilt in the photo includes a wider mixture and placement of both prints and plaids.)

Quilt Top:

Light Prints: 35 scraps, minimum size about 12" square, OR ⅛ yard each of 35 fabrics.

Dark Prints: Same as Light Prints.

Stripes or Plaids: Same as Light Prints.

Borders: 3¼ yards dark green solid, 3 yards beige solid.

Binding: Use the remaining fabric from the prints and plaids above.

Backing: 6½ yards of good quality unbleached muslin.

Batting: 90" x 108" (queen size) bonded polyester batt.

OTHER SUPPLIES

- Iron
- Material for templates
- Marking pencils or soap chips
- Scissors (for paper and fabric)
- Rulers
- Thread for piecing
- Pins
- Large 45/90 degree plastic triangle
- Thread or safety pins for basting
- Quilting needles
- Two spools natural-color quilting thread
- Thimble
- Long straightedge
- Hoop or frame for quilting

READY TO WORK

COLOR AND FABRIC KEY
L = Light Print
D = Dark Print
S = Stripe or Plaid
G = Dark Green
B = Beige

TEMPLATES

Begin by making templates of the two Spools pattern pieces: Square (Template 1) and Trapezoid (Template 2). Mark the grain lines on each template. Note that ¼" seams must be added on all sides of each piece.

CUTTING

Begin with the Light Prints (L) and cut eight each of the trapezoid from each of the 35 fabrics. Continue with the Dark Prints (D) and cut eight each of the trapezoid from each of the 35 dark print fabrics.

Continue with the Stripes or Plaids (S). Use the square and cut four each from the 35 fabrics. Be careful to place grain lines so that the stripes or plaids are on grain.

Cut the following border pieces from the Dark Green (G) fabric (includes allowances for seams and mitering):

For inner borders – Cut two sides 3½" x 90½" and cut two ends 3½" x 66½".

For outer borders – Cut two sides 4½" x 102½" and cut two ends 4½" x 78½".

From the Solid Beige (B) fabric, cut the following borders (includes allowances for seams and mitering):

Cut two sides 2½" x 94½"
Cut two ends 2½" x 70½"

PUTTING IT TOGETHER

BLOCK PIECING

Refer to Diagram 1 for the basic Spool pattern, which consists of five pieces. Arrange the five pieces according to the diagram, with the stripes going across as indicated by the arrow.

If you are using a plaid fabric, designate a dominant plaid or color and place it according to the arrow.

Begin piecing by stitching a Light (L) trapezoid on each side of the center Stripe (S) fabric, as in Diagram 2. Complete the unit by joining the two Dark Print (D) trapezoids in pivot seams as shown in Diagram 3.

Complete four 6" units. Then

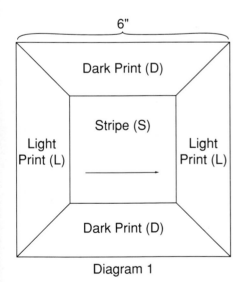

Diagram 1

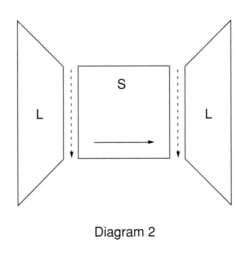

Diagram 2

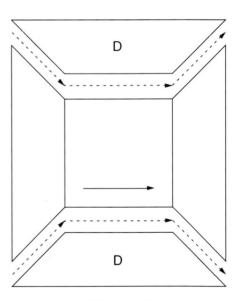

Diagram 3

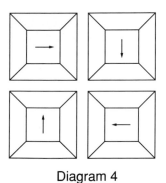

Diagram 4

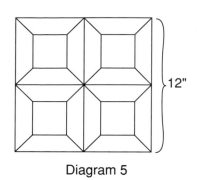

12"

Diagram 5

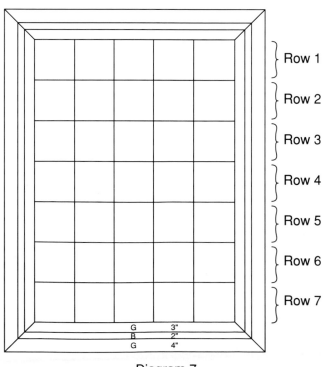

Diagram 6

Diagram 7

Row 1

Row 2

Row 3

Row 4

Row 5

Row 6

Row 7

G   3"
B   2"
G   4"

arrange these with the stripes running in a clockwise sequence in the four directions, as illustrated by the arrows in Diagram 4. If you are using plaids, you may designate a dominant plaid or color and place it in the four directions.

Stitch the four blocks together to complete the 12" block as shown in Diagram 5.

Make 35, 12" blocks in a similar fashion.

ASSEMBLY AND BORDERS

Lay the 35 blocks in five rows and seven columns on a large flat surface. Place them in a suitable color arrangement. Join the five blocks that make up Row 1 in short vertical seams, as shown in Diagram 6. Similarly, piece Rows 2 through 7. Join these rows in long horizontal seams.

To complete the top, add the dark green and beige borders. First stitch the 3" inner green borders. Next, attach the 2" middle beige borders. Last, add the 4" outer green border. Use the large 45/90-degree triangle to mark and miter the corners.

THE FINISHING TOUCH

QUILTING

From the 6½ yards of muslin backing fabric, cut two 3¼ yard lengths. Keep one intact (about 42" wide). Split the other piece into two 21" widths. Join a split width to each side of the intact center panel. Press the seams toward the outside.

Place the quilt backing right side down on a large, flat surface. Smooth the batting over it. Place the pressed quilt top over the batting, right side up. Pin or thread-baste the three layers together for quilting.

Using natural-color quilting thread, quilt "in-the-ditch" close to the seam (on the opposite side of where the seams are pressed), around each piece, as suggested in Diagram 8. Use a large triangle and a washable marker or soap chip to mark parallel diagonal lines at about 1½" intervals, across the three borders, as suggested in Diagram 8. Quilt the marked lines.

BINDING

Trim the batting to ½" larger than the quilt top, to allow for filler in the binding. Trim the backing to match the top.

From the remaining light and dark print fabrics cut 90 trapezoids (Template 2). Piece these (with alternating lights and darks) in lengths to extend along the sides and ends of the quilt – about 25 trapezoids for each side, and about 20 trapezoids for each end. Use Diagram 9 as a guide for piecing.

Place the pieced binding on the quilt front with right sides together and raw edges even. Stitch in a ¼" seam through all four layers. Turn under ¼" along the remaining raw edge of the binding. Turn the binding to the back and whipstitch it in place.

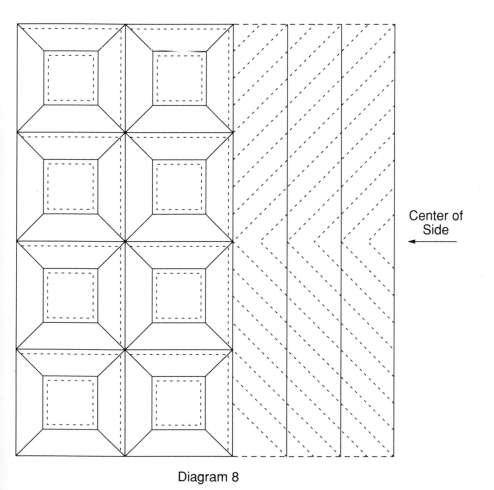

Center of
Side

Diagram 8

Diagram 9

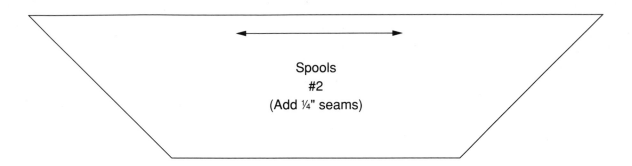

Spools
#2
(Add ¼" seams)

Spools
#1
(Add ¼" seams)

Variations created using the Spool design.

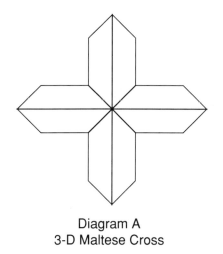

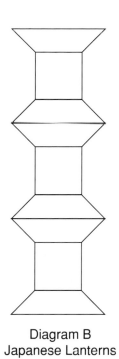

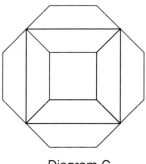

Diagram A
3-D Maltese Cross

Diagram B
Japanese Lanterns

Diagram C
Large Octagon Pattern

QUILTED TO A "T"
(MIXED-T)
Quilt by Pat Simonsen, Eau Claire, Wisconsin

QUILTED TO A "T"

The Mixed-T quilt is a marvelous and colorful way to combine a variety of fabrics. Pat Simonsen selected a combination of ten fabrics against a light background for her crib-size quilt. If you prefer to use only two colors, the design will be boldly abstract. If you mix lots of odds and ends from your scrap bag, the piece will be especially colorful, and economical.

QUILTED TO A "T" is Pat's second Mixed-T quilt. She made her first one when she first began quilting several years ago. She used fabric scraps from years of home sewing projects undertaken by herself and her three daughters. It was truly "scrap" in flavor, including every color imaginable in fine prints, solids, geometrics, and ginghams. It was the sense of abandon that Pat used in her piecing and assembly that made the quilt especially design-appealing.

That first quilt was used on her daughter's bed for many years. Put to practical use, it eventually became well-worn. Pat has recently been seen with needle and thread, carefully replacing worn out "T's" with freshly cut patches.

Pat's second Mixed-T quilt, pictured here, was made as a crib quilt to celebrate the birth of Megan Shavalier. The combination of pastel prints and solids in rainbow soft colors is perfect for a child's quilt.

The Mixed-T is an uncomplicated pattern. The worksheet resembles a series of rectangular columns, every other column with slanted lines. There are only two templates – a rectangle and a trapezoid which is reversed for half of the pieces. The top is assembled in horizontal rows. Piecing is not difficult, but attention must be paid to the placement of inverted rows.

Portions of the pattern could be converted to quick techniques. For those who prefer speed cutting and piecing, some parts can be converted into strip assembly. (Example: Imagine the large rectangles as a vertical column of ten colors – blue, white, green, white, yellow, white, peach, white, lavender and white. These rectangles could be cut as wide panels of color, stitched together, re-cut into columns, and inserted between the narrower pieced columns.)

The pattern can easily be enlarged for a youth/twin or full/queen bed. Simply stitch additional "T's" to either end of the rows and attach more rows at the top or bottom. The design is built for easy expansion.

Your name doesn't have to begin with the letter "T" to make this quilt. And you don't have to be from Texas, Tennessee, or Timbuktu. But just in case you answer to a name like Thelma or Tchaikowsky, I've included nine additional design variations on the letter "T" (page 107). These are generally more detailed and include Four-, Seven-, and Nine-Patch variations such as the Capitol T, Double T, T-Square, T-Quartette, and Imperial T. Some are set in spiral fashion, others in a diagonal or medallion setting. All have great potential for a mixture of fabrics and arrangements. How about a "T" sampler?

Pat opted for no-frills hand quilting – diagonal lines that make an "X" formation on each large rectangle. These clean lines combine and flow well with the angular piecing.

If you suspect you've seen or read about Pat's quilts before, you probably have. Two of her quilts, a computer-generated appliqué design and a holiday wall quilt are featured in my book, *A Collection of Favorite Quilts: Narratives, Patterns, and Directions for 15 Quilts.* Other patterns by Pat have been published in *Quilter's Newsletter Magazine,* the *'89 Quilt Art Engagement Calendar,* and the book *Award-Winning Quick Quilts.*

MIXED-T QUILT

FOR STARTERS

The following list will help you enjoy a smooth start and steady progress in your work on the Mixed-T quilt. It contains a variety of general information about making the quilt.

- Wash and press all fabrics before you begin.
- Ten different pastel prints or solids are suggested.
- A mixture of fabric scraps would be an excellent alternative.
- All seams are ¼".
- For templates (patterns of the quilt pieces) use sturdy plastic, cardboard, or sandpaper, and be sure to note grain lines.
- Piecing may be done by hand or machine. For hand piecing, make the templates without seam allowances, and add them when marking and cutting the fabrics.

For machine piecing, include the ¼" seam allowances on the templates.

- Mixed-T is constructed in horizontal rows.
- Each pieced "T" unit measures 6" x 5", finished.
- All "background" areas are white.
- The finished size for the Mixed-T quilt is 42" x 50".

SUPPLIES

Use 44"/45" wide cotton or cotton polyester blends.

Quilt Top:

Pastel Prints or Solids: ⅛ yard EACH of ten fabrics in colors including blue, pink, lavender, green, and yellow, OR ten scrap fabrics, minimum size each about 15" square.

White: 1½ yards

Binding: ¾ yard medium blue.
Backing: 1⅝ yards white.
Batting: Use a 45" x 60" (crib-size) bonded polyester batt.

OTHER SUPPLIES

- Iron
- Material for templates
- Marking pencils or soap chips
- Scissors (for paper and fabric)
- Rulers
- Thread for piecing
- Pins
- Thread or safety pins for basting
- Quilting needles
- One spool white quilting thread
- Thimble
- Long straightedge
- Hoop or frame for quilting

READY TO WORK

COLOR AND FABRIC KEY
P = Pastel (print or solid)
W = White
R = Reverse template

TEMPLATES

Begin by making templates of both Mixed-T pattern pieces – a rectangle (Template 1), and a trapezoid (Template 2). Mark the grain lines on each template. Note also that ¼" seams must be added on all sides of each piece. Note that Template 2 (trapezoid) must be reversed for half of the pieces cut. These reverse pieces are designated with the letter "R" in the instructions and diagrams.

CUTTING

Begin with the Pastel (P) fabrics. From EACH of the ten fabrics, cut the following pieces:

Cut five of Template 1 (rectangle).

Cut ten of Template 2 (trapezoid), half of which must be cut with the template reversed (5R). (Note that you will have an extra rectangle for half of the pastel fabrics. Add these to your scrap basket.) Continue with the White (W) fabric and cut the following pieces:

Cut 45 of Template l (rectangle).

Cut 100 of Template 2 (trapezoid), half of them reverse (50R).

PUTTING IT TOGETHER

PIECING

The Mixed-T quilt is constructed by horizontal rows, as shown in Diagram 1. Refer to Diagram 2 for an illustration of the basic "T" unit. The position of the "T" unit changes from row to row. Odd-numbered rows have colored "T's" in an upright position. Even-numbered rows have colored "T's" in an inverted position.

Start with the pastel fabric for the top row of the quilt. Piece a Pastel (P) trapezoid to a White (W) trapezoid, as in Diagram 3. Next, piece a Pastel Reverse trapezoid

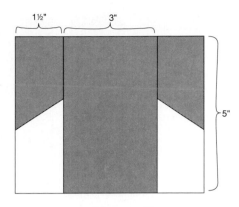

Diagram 2

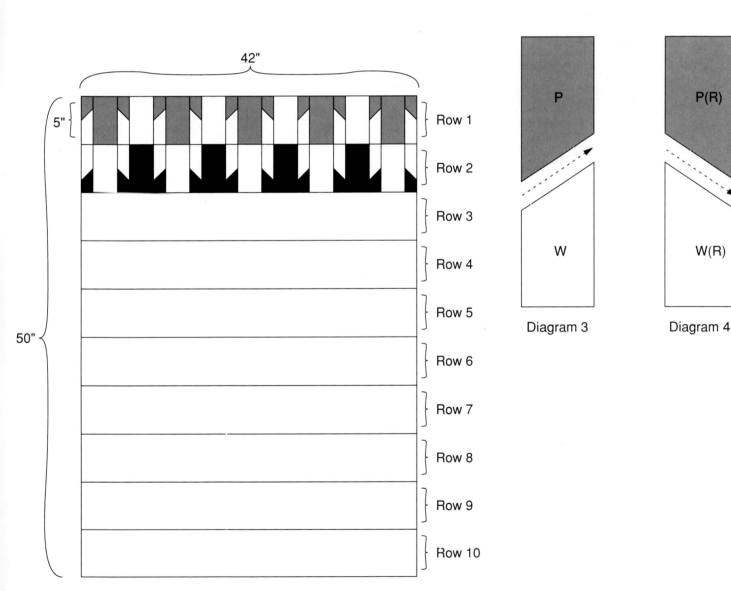

Diagram 1

Diagram 3

Diagram 4

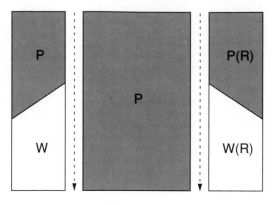

Diagram 5

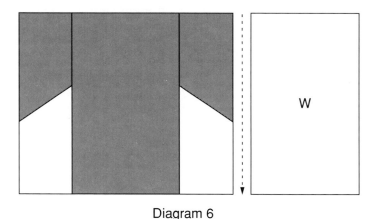

Diagram 6

(PR) to a White Reverse trapezoid (WR), as in Diagram 4. Make five of each of these units.

Complete the "T" by adding a Pastel (P) rectangle between the trapezoid units, as in Diagram 5. Make five of these units.

Next, add a White (W) rectangle to the "T" as in Diagram 6. Continue adding pastel "T's" and white rectangles to complete Row 1, as illustrated in Diagram 7. Row 31 is composed of five pastel "T's" and 4 white rectangles.

Press all the seams in Row 1 to the same side.

Select the fabrics for Rows 3, 5, 7, and 9 (odd-numbered rows). Make horizontal panels similar to Row 1, using the steps and diagrams outlined above. Press the seams in the odd-numbered rows in the same direction as Row 1.

For Row 2 (and all the even-numbered rows) use a similar piecing procedure EXCEPT note that the pastel and white fabrics are in opposite positions, as shown in Diagram 8. Begin with the fabric

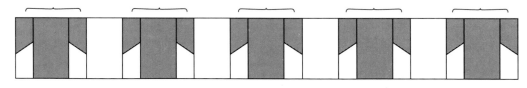

Diagram 7

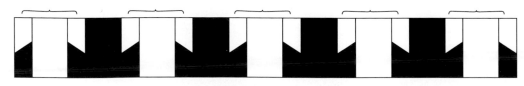

Diagram 8

designated for Row 2. Complete the row (five white "T's" and four pastel rectangles). Make similar horizontal panels for Rows 4, 6, 8, and 10.

Press all the seams in the even-numbered rows in the opposite direction of the odd-numbered rows.

ASSEMBLY

Place the 10 rows in order. Piece Row 1 to Row 2 in a horizontal seam as shown in Diagram 9. Continue adding Rows 3 through 10 to complete the top.

THE FINISHING TOUCH

QUILTING

Place the 1⅝ yard of white backing fabric right side down on a flat surface. Smooth the batting over it. Place the pressed quilt top over the batting, right side up. Pin or thread-baste the three layers together for quilting. Use a long straightedge and a washable marking pencil or soap chip to mark the quilting lines suggested in Diagram 10 ("X's" on all the rectangles). Quilt with white thread.

BINDING

Trim the batting to ½" larger than the quilt top, to allow for filler in the binding. Trim the backing to match the top. From the ¾ yard of medium blue binding fabric, make 3" wide continuous-bias binding.

Fold the binding in half lengthwise, wrong sides together. Then stitch it to the quilt front in a seam that penetrates all the layers. Turn the binding to the back of the quilt and whipstitch it in place.

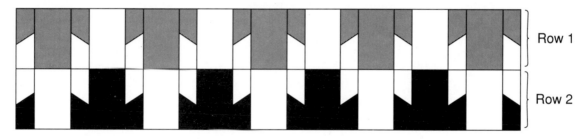

Diagram 9

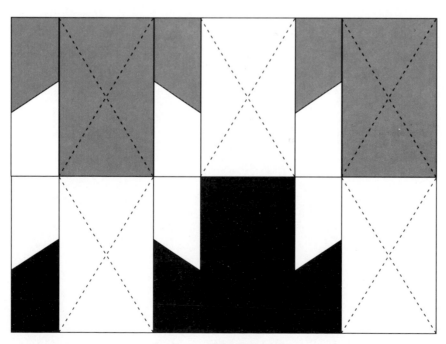

Diagram 10

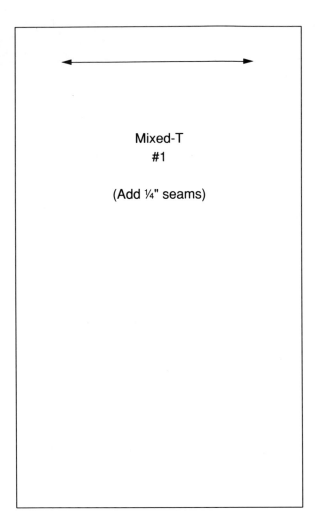

Mixed-T
#1

(Add ¼" seams)

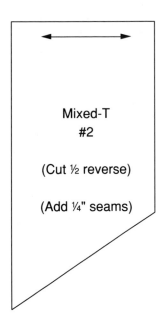

Mixed-T
#2

(Cut ½ reverse)

(Add ¼" seams)

"T" Block Variations

  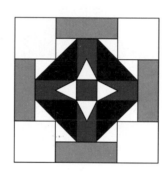

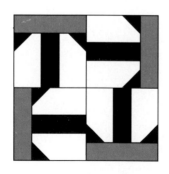 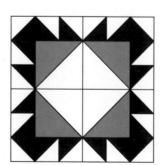 

AROUND THE WORLD AND ACROSS THE GENERATIONS
(TRIP AROUND THE WORLD)
Quilt by Dorothy Gilbertson, Eau Claire, Wisconsin

AROUND THE WORLD AND ACROSS THE GENERATIONS

Trip Around The World is a long-time favorite pattern. It is often seen as rows of squares radiating outward from lightest to darkest. The color sequences may be repeated any number of times and in various combinations to make any size quilt, from crib- to king-size.

Dorothy Gilbertson's crib quilt is made entirely from cotton flannel fabrics, so it's soft and cuddly, perfect for a baby or small child. Most adults I know wouldn't mind having it spread across their lap or bed, or around their shoulders, either.

The assortment of flannel fabrics that Dorothy used spans more than two generations. Several fabrics date from her early quiltmaking days when her children were toddlers. Some fabrics may be even older than that, shared from her own mother's scrap bag. Fabrics used in the outer areas of the quilt are more recent purchases.

Dorothy started piecing AROUND THE WORLD AND ACROSS THE GENERATIONS over 30 years ago. It was originally intended for her son, Paul, then a toddler. Dorothy cut and pieced tiny squares of flannel, carefully highlighting the juvenile designs such as animals, nursery-rhyme characters, and playthings on each square. Dorothy had nearly completed the top when the progress was interrupted and the unfinished piece was set aside and eventually packed away.

About 30 years later, when her first grandchild was expected, Dorothy unpacked the top and resumed piecing. She added squares to the incomplete outer green border and appliquéd the top to light flannel borders, to square off the edges. She hand-quilted around each piece and diagonally through selected rows of squares. AROUND THE WORLD was completed in time for her grandson, Joseph Paul Gilbertson.

What sets Dorothy's quilt apart is her careful selection of the juvenile design motifs on each fabric. Each row of squares features a thoughtfully centered design such as puppies, kittens, and mice; musical instruments and toys; and circles and polka dots. This systematic arrangement of shapes and colors lends a perfect rectangular "framing" effect.

Careful attention to detail makes this an especially attractive child's quilt. An array of soft flannel pastels makes it nearly irresistible. Chances are good that you, too, know a child that wouldn't mind snuggling up in a quilt like Dorothy's.

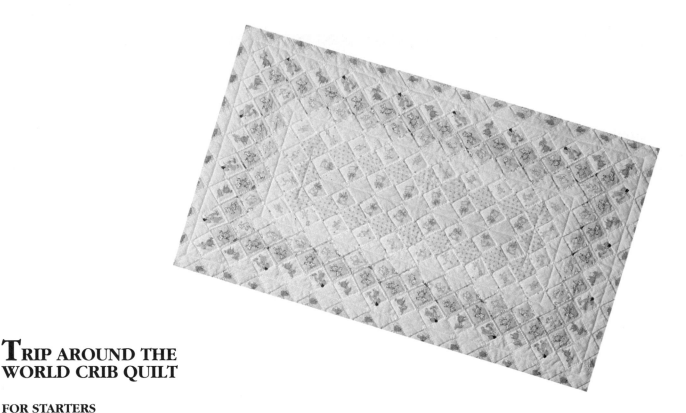

TRIP AROUND THE WORLD CRIB QUILT

FOR STARTERS

The following list will help you enjoy a smooth start and steady progress in your work on the Trip Around the World quilt. It contains a variety of general information about making the quilt:

- Wash and press all fabrics before you begin.
- Flannel fabrics, including both solids and prints, in soft pastel colors are recommended.
- A mixture of scrap fabrics is a good alternative.
- All seams are ¼".
- Use sturdy plastic, cardboard, or sandpaper to make the square template.
- Piecing may be done by hand or machine. For hand piecing, make the template without seam allowances, and add them when marking and cutting the fabrics. For machine piecing, include the ¼" seam allowances on the template.
- Only one pattern piece, a 2" square (finished), is required.

- Trip Around the World is pieced in diagonal rows and assembled in three large diagonal sections.
- The pieced section is appliquéd to a light-flannel border.
- Two sets of instructions are given for this quilt. One is for the quilt using fabrics like the pictured quilt. The other is for an optional design using an array of 15 different fabrics. Watch for special notes, indicated with an asterisk (*) for the optional instructions.
- The finished size for the Trip Around the World crib quilt is 48" by 65".

SUPPLIES

Use 44"/45" wide cotton or cotton blend flannel.

*If you plan to make your quilt like the one pictured, use the following yardage amounts. If you prefer to use a different array of 15 fabrics, disregard these yardage suggestions. Instead, refer ahead to the Fabric Number Yardage Chart which is included on page 111.

Quilt Top:

Light Solids:
  Blue: ⅛ yard
  Pink: ⅛ yard
  Yellow: ½ yard
  Light Green: ½ yard
  Medium Green: ½ yard

Light Prints or Juvenile Prints:
  (If you use juvenile prints and plan to center the figures or designs, as in the photograph, you must increase the print fabric yardages. Doubling the amount listed would be a good suggestion.)
  Pink Print 1: ⅛ yard
  Green Print: ¼ yard
  Pink Print 2: 1¼ yard
  Blue Print: ¼ yard
  White Print: ¼ yard
  Pink Print 3: ⅜ yard
  Yellow Print: ⅜ yard
  Polka Dot: ½ yard
  Pink Print 4: ½ yard

Borders and Binding: Buy two yards of light print flannel.

Backing: Four yards of flannel fabric in a light solid color of your choice.

Batting: Use a 72" x 90" (twin size) bonded polyester batt.

*Optional Yardage Chart by Fabric Number (15 fabrics, including center fabrics):

Center: ⅛ yard
Row 1: ⅛ yard
Row 2: ¼ yard
Row 3: ¼ yard
Row 4: ¼ yard
Row 5: ¼ yard
Row 6: ¼ yard
Row 7: ¼ yard
Row 8: ⅜ yard
Row 9: ⅜ yard
Row 10: ⅜ yard
Row 11: ½ yard
Row 12: ½ yard
Row 13: ½ yard
Row 14: ½ yard

OTHER SUPPLIES
- Iron
- Material for templates
- Marking pencils or soap chips
- Scissors (for paper and scissors)
- Rulers
- Thread for piecing
- Pins
- Light green thread for appliqué
- Thread or safety pins for basting
- Quilting needles
- Two spools light green quilting thread
- Thimble
- Long straightedge
- Hoop or frame for quilting

READY TO WORK
COLOR AND FABRIC KEY
Solids:
B = Blue
P = Pink
Y = Yellow
LG = Light Green
MG = Medium Green

Pastels:
Pl = Pink Print l
GP = Green Print
P2 = Pink Print 2
BP = Blue Print
WP = White Print
P3 = Pink Print 3
YP = Yellow Print
PD = Polka Dot
P4 = Pink Print 4

TEMPLATE
Make a sturdy template of the 2" square pattern piece. Mark the grain line on the template. Note that ¼" seams must be added on all sides.

CUTTING
The fabrics in the Trip Around the World quilt are designated by both letters and numbers. If you are making your quilt like the one in the photo, you should refer to the fabric letter designations (B for Blue, P2 for Pink Print 2, etc.).

Begin with the Solid fabrics and cut the following squares:

Blue (B): Cut four (for quilt center).

Pink (P): Cut three (for quilt center).

Yellow (Y): Cut 64 (for Rows 2 and 8).

Light Green (LG): Cut 72 (for Rows 4 and 10).

Medium Green (MG): Cut 68 (for Row 14).

From the Light Print border fabric, cut the following pieces:

Cut two side borders 6½" x 66".

Cut two end borders 6½" x 50".

Continue with the Print fabrics and cut the following number of squares:

Pl: Cut 16 (for Row l)
GP: Cut 24 (for Row 3)
P2: Cut 32 (for Row 5)
BP: Cut 36 (for Row 6)
WP: Cut 40 (for Row 7)
P3: Cut 48 (for Row 9)
YP: Cut 56 (for Row 11)
PD: Cut 60 (for Row 12)

P4: Cut 64 (for Row 13)

*If you are using 15 different fabrics, it will be easier to refer to the fabric number designations (1 through 14), shown in Diagram 1, and proceed ahead to the following cutting chart by fabric and row numbers.

Then cut the following number of squares:

Center (C): Cut 7
Row 1: Cut 16
Row 2: Cut 20
Row 3: Cut 24
Row 4: Cut 28
Row 5: Cut 32
Row 6: Cut 36
Row 7: Cut 40
Row 8: Cut 44
Row 9: Cut 48
Row 10: Cut 52
Row 11: Cut 56
Row 12: Cut 60
Row 13: Cut 64
Row 14: Cut 68
PIECING

Think of the Trip Around the World quilt as constructed in three large diagonal sections, as shown in Diagram 2. The two corner triangular sections are the same.

*If you are using 15 different fabrics, use Diagram 1 as your guide for placement of pieces and order of piecing. Use row numbers instead of fabric letters for the piecing directions.

Begin construction with the center oblong diagonal section. Begin with the center fabric, a Pink Solid (P) and add Pink Print 1 (P1) squares on opposite sides, as in Diagram 3. Continue adding fabrics on each side, referring to the fabric letter code in Diagram 4, until you have added 14 squares on each side of the center square. Your completed strip will have 29 squares.

Make two more strips starting with a Pink Solid (P) center, as before.

Next, make two strips starting with a Blue Solid (B) center.

Arrange these five strips according to Diagram 5, with the ends staggered and the pink and blue centers alternating. Then piece these strips together in four long seams, to complete the center section of the quilt.

Refer to Diagram 6 for a corner section. Begin by piecing the longest strip (29 squares) with the Blue Solid (B) center, as described above. Notice that the number of squares in each strip diminishes by two squares in each row as you move toward the corner, where there is only one square.

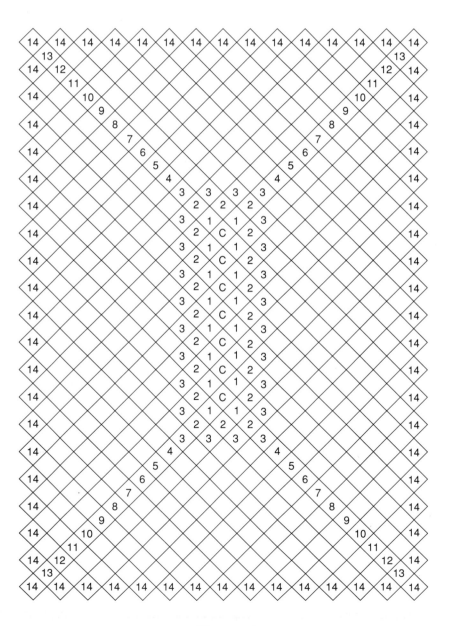

Diagram 1

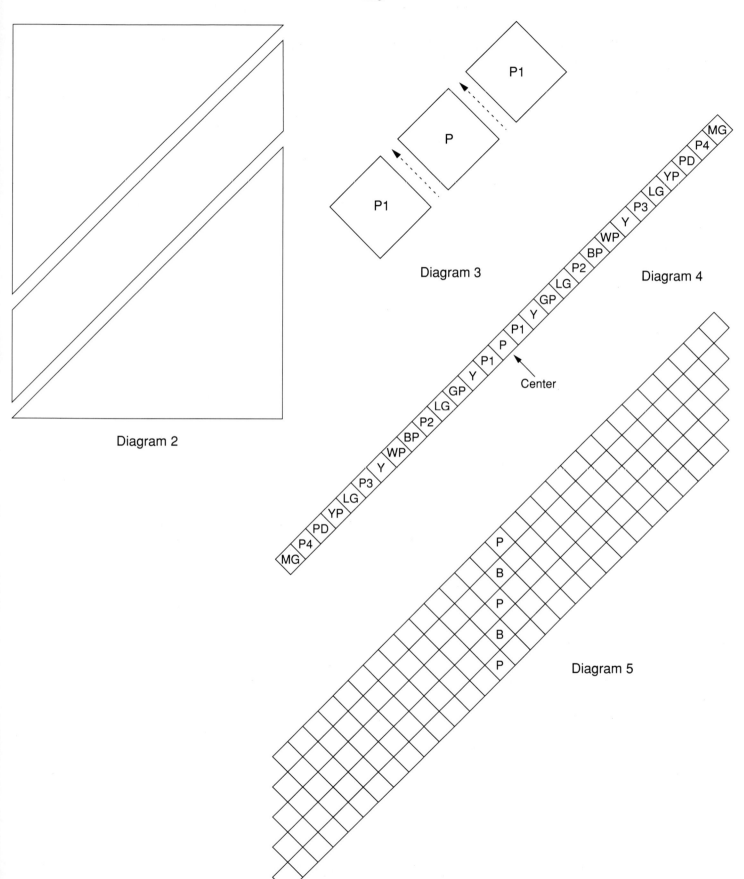

Diagram 2

Diagram 3

Diagram 4

Center

Diagram 5

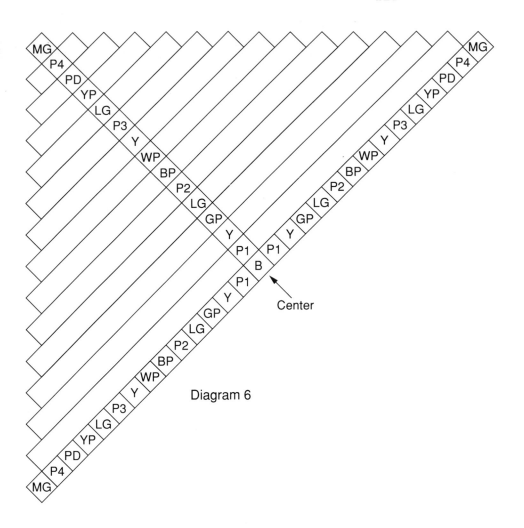

Diagram 6

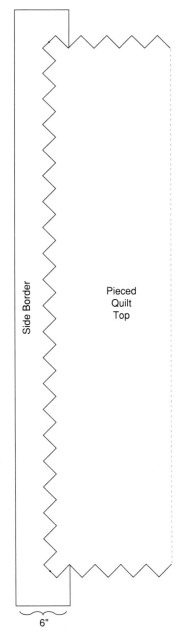

Side Border

Pieced Quilt Top

6"

Diagram 7

Piece the second strip, which has a Pink Print 1 (P1) in the middle and continues with the other 13 fabrics added on each side. This strip will have 27 squares.

Continue piecing the remaining strips. You will have a total of 14 pieced strips, each successively smaller than the previous, plus a single solid Medium Green (MG) square for the corner.

Arrange all 14 strips and the single corner square according to Diagram 6. Then join them in long seams to complete a corner section of the quilt.

Make a similar triangular section for the opposite corner of the quilt.

Join the three sections together to complete the center of the quilt,

referring back to Diagram 2.

*If you are using 15 different fabrics, use Diagram 1 as your guide and follow steps similar to those above, using fabric numbers instead of letters as a guide.

BORDERS

Turn under ¼" on all of the outside squares. Press the turned edges. Place the top over the side border, as in Diagram 7. Pin in place. Then appliqué the edge of the pieced top to the side border with tiny stitches. Begin and end the appliqué stitches at the dot markings.

Appliqué the opposite side of the quilt to the other side border.

Next, add the end borders. Pin the pressed quilt edge to the border and miter the corners over the side border pieces. Appliqué in place to complete the quilt top. Trim the excess border fabric from behind the mitered corners.

THE FINISHING TOUCH

QUILTING

From the four yards of backing fabric, cut two 2-yard lengths. Keep one intact (about 42" wide). From the other piece, cut two 6" widths. Join a 6" width to each side of the intact center panel. Press the seams toward the outside.

Place the quilt backing right side down on a large, flat surface. Smooth the batting over it. Place the pressed quilt top over the batting, right side up. Pin or thread-baste the three layers together for quilting.

Use a washable marking pencil and a straightedge to mark the quilting lines suggested in Diagram 8. Use light green quilting thread to quilt around all the squares, about ¼" away from the seams. Quilt a line through the center of the squares in every other row, and a diagonal cross hatching pattern in the borders, as shown in Diagram 8.

BINDING

Trim the batting to ½" larger than the quilt top, to allow for filler in the binding. Trim the backing to match the top. From the 1 yard of light print binding fabric, make 3" wide continuous bias binding.

Fold the binding in half lengthwise, wrong sides together. Then attach it to the quilt front in a seam that penetrates all the layers. Turn the binding to the back and whipstitch it in place.

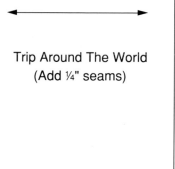

Trip Around The World
(Add ¼" seams)

Diagram 8

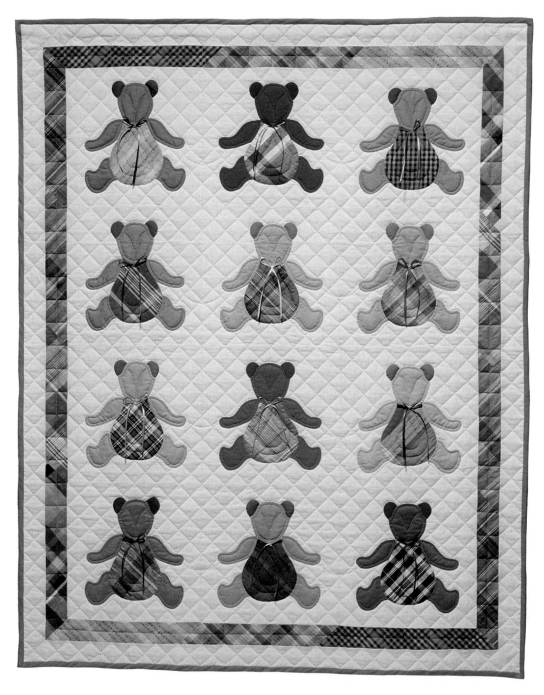

BOW TIE BEARS
(TEDDY BEAR APPLIQUÉ)
Quilt by the Author

BOW TIE BEARS

When I decided to combine my current interest in plaid fabrics and appliqué design, I looked for a simple pattern with general appeal. I wanted additional ideas and samples for my "Plaids: Who said You Can't Use Them In Quilts?" workshop, specifically something appliqué, so why not teddy bears? Besides, almost everybody likes bears. Nobody warned me that as I selected each fabric, dressed each bear, and stitched each arm, leg, and ear that I would end up with something "cute," which is not the direction I thought my quiltmaking was headed.

Like previous projects, the fabrics were chosen carefully – 12 plaids from people or places that I wanted to spotlight or remember – a swatch of nubby green plaid from an Australian quiltmaker, a piece of coarsely woven kikoy cloth from Kenya, a swatch from a workshop participant in Chicago, and a scrap from my sister Jean. I had collected fabrics from as near as Chippewa Falls, Wisconsin, to as far as Victoria, Australia. A wide range of colors was included – bright cheery ones that would appeal to the child in all of us. Solid fabrics in light and dark colors compatible with the highlighted plaids were chosen. Each bear retains its own personality in coloration and outfit, complete with a satin ribbon bow tie to match.

I admit that the design is not very innovative. Really, anybody can design a teddy bear. Mine was adapted from a tiny graphic illustration in a news tabloid. I favored the notion of a cuddly bear, one you would want to reach out and hug. (As I adapted the design it became so rounded and cuddly that it soon appeared pot-bellied or pregnant, which is not what I was looking for.)

My test block was overly round and included many tedious details such as hand and foot pads, appliquéd eyes, nose, and mouth, all of which looked all right but seemed to detract from the simplicity of the shape and the unique plaid fabric in each bear. So I settled on a simpler design without added details, leaving those to the imagination of each viewer and quiltmaker.

Each bear rests against a plain muslin background. The 12 bears are enclosed with a pieced border cut from bias strips of selected plaids used in the bears. These strips are arranged in a gradual dark-to-light sequence from two corners of the quilt. Careful attention was required to piece and attach the borders to avoid distortion of the bias edges. The outer light borders and quilting lines added the necessary stability.

Each bear is dressed up with a double-faced satin ribbon bow tie and decorative quilting that highlights the body parts. A gently curved line of quilting connects each bear hand-in-hand with its neighbor.

So here they are – colorful, cuddly, and yes, even cute – poised to deliver comfort and pleasure to child, parent, and grandparent alike. If you haven't already done so, gather your cheeriest fabrics and join in the teddy bear mania.

BOW TIE BEARS

FOR STARTERS

The following will help you enjoy a smooth start and steady progress in your work on the Bow Tie Bears quilt. It contains a variety of general information about making the quilt.

- Wash and press all fabrics before you begin.
- Twelve different plaid fabrics are needed for the bears and the pieced border.
- Twelve light and medium colors and 12 coordinating dark solid colors are needed for the appliqué.
- Scant ¼" seams are recommended for the turn-under allowance on appliqué pieces.
- Use ¼" seams for piecing the blocks and borders.
- For templates (patterns of the quilt pieces) use sturdy plastic, cardboard, or sandpaper, and be sure to note grain lines.
- The Bow Tie Bears require hand appliqué. Use the method of your choice. Instructions for a simple and dependable freezer-paper appliqué method are included.
- 12 appliqué blocks are required.
- Each appliquéd block measures 12" square, finished.
- The pieced plaid bias border and outer muslin borders are each 2" wide.
- The finished size for the Bow Tie Bears quilt is 44" by 56".

SUPPLIES

Use 44"/45" wide cotton or cotton polyester blends.

Quilt Top:

Plaids: 12 different plaid fabrics are required. Seven of these plaids are also used in the pieced border.

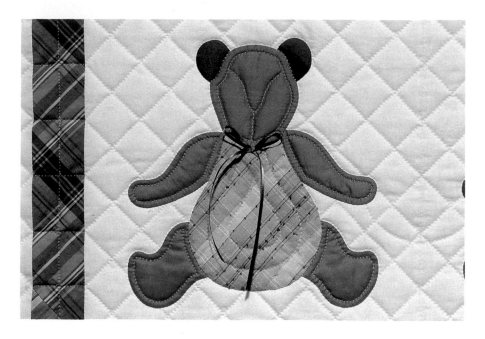

Additional fabric is needed for these seven border plaids. For the seven plaids that will also be used in the border, buy ⅜ yard each. For the remaining five plaids, ¼ yard is sufficient. If you use scraps for the body of the bear, the minimum size needed is a piece about 7" square.

Light Solids (head, arms, and legs): ⅛ yard each of 12 colors to match the plaids. If you use scraps, the minimum size is a piece about 8" square.

Dark Solids (ears): 12 different colors to coordinate with the Light Solids above. A small piece about 3" square is needed. For new yardage, you need to buy ⅛ yard of each color.

Unbleached Muslin: 4 yards of good quality muslin.

Binding: 1 yard of Teal.

Backing: Included in Unbleached Muslin above.

Batting: Use a 45" x 60" (crib size) bonded polyester batt.

Ribbon: ½ yard each of 12 colors of ¼" wide double-faced satin ribbon (colors to match the 12 plaids above).

OTHER SUPPLIES

- Iron
- Material for templates
- Freezer paper
- Marking pencils or soap chips
- Scissors (for paper and fabric)
- Rulers
- Thread for piecing
- Thread for appliqué in colors to match the plaids and light and dark solid fabrics
- Pins
- Thread or safety pins for basting
- Quilting needles
- One spool natural-color quilting thread
- Thimble
- Long straightedge
- Hoop or frame for quilting
- Appliqué scissors (optional)
- Invisible nylon thread
- Protractor

READY TO WORK

FABRIC KEY
P = Plaid
L = Light Solid
D = Dark Solid
M = Unbleached Muslin

BACKGROUND BLOCKS,
BORDERS, AND BACKING

Fabric for the background blocks, borders, and quilt backing are included in the four yards of unbleached muslin. Refer to Diagram 1 for a suggested cutting layout.

Begin by cutting two panels, each about 25" x 60". Label and set these aside for the quilt backing.

Next, cut the following outer border pieces (allowances for seams and mitering included):

Cut two side borders 2½" x 56½".

Cut two end borders 2½" x 44½".

Next, cut the 12 background blocks, each 12½" x 12½" including seams. Each background block should measure at least 12½" from raw edge to raw edge. It is recommended that background blocks be cut slightly larger (e.g., 13") and trimmed to 12½" after the appliqué is completed. This extra tolerance will allow for any shrinkage resulting from the appliqué's stitching and for raveling from routine handling.

TEMPLATES

Make templates of all five Bow Tie Bear parts: Body (1), Arm (2), Leg (3), Head (4), and Ear (5). Mark the suggested grain lines on each template. Mark the dots, which will be used to locate the pieces onto the background blocks.

Although grain line is not a crucial factor in all appliqué, it is a notable part of the design in this Bear pattern. Each plaid body is set with the plaids running in diagonal directions. The grain line in the solid pieces (head, arms, legs, and ears) is suggested mainly to lend some consistency among the pieces. Variant grain lines may be distracting in some solid fabrics.

Note that scant ¼" seam allowances (actually about ³⁄₁₆") must be added on all sides of each appliqué piece.

PUTTING IT TOGETHER

FREEZER-PAPER APPLIQUÉ

This method works well on the gentle curves of the Bow Tie Bears. If you have never attempted a freezer-paper method, it is recommended that you do a test block first.

Cut a piece of freezer paper about 10" square. Note that one side is shiny, the other side is dull. Place the freezer paper (shiny side down) on a flat surface. Begin with the body of the bear. Place the Template 1 on the freezer paper and trace around it, without adding seam allowances. Continue to trace the other parts of a bear. For each bear, you will need to trace one body, one head, two legs (reverse the template for one leg), two arms (reverse the template for one arm), and two ears (reverse the template for one ear).

Use your paper scissors to cut the eight pieces out exactly as traced.

Next, place each freezer paper piece shiny side down on the wrong side of the selected fabric. Place the body on the Plaid (P) fabric. Place the head, legs, and arms on the Light Solid (L) fabric, and the ears on the Dark Solid (D) fabric. See Diagram 2 for color and fabric placement.

NOTE: Generally, with the solid fabrics, and with most woven plaids, there will be no distinguishable right or wrong side. If you are using printed plaids (design appears only on one side, so they are not reversible), the wrong side is easily noted.

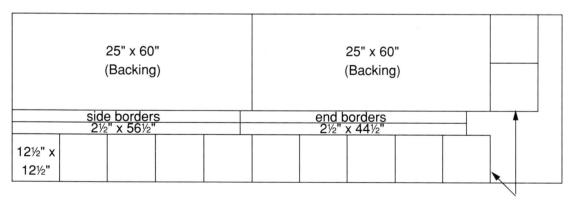

Diagram 1

Some care should be given to placement on the plaid fabrics, depending on whether or not you want to get the diagonal effect in the pictured quilt.

Use a hot iron and gently press the paper pattern to the fabric. Hold the iron in place for a few seconds until the paper adheres firmly. Let the paper and fabric cool. Then cut around the shape, carefully adding the scant ³⁄₁₆" turn-under allowance all around. If you add too much allowance, it will be bulky and cumbersome to turn under smoothly.

Continue to press the pattern pieces until you have all eight parts for a bear.

Fold the background block into quarters horizontally, vertically, and diagonally, as in Diagram 3. Press lightly to mark the divisions. Refer to Diagram 4 for placement of the appliqué pieces. Place the body of the bear on the background square, placing the marked dot in the center of the square, as in Diagram 5. Pin it in place. Next, locate the leg positions by matching the dots on the diagonal creases, as in Diagram 6. The leg pieces will be tucked underneath the body piece. Pin the legs in place.

Also locate the arm positions by matching the dots on the horizontal creases. The arm pieces will be tucked underneath the body piece. Pin the arm pieces in place. Be sure that both arms and legs are sufficiently tucked beneath the main body piece so that the turned-under edge of the body will adequately cover the raw edges and allowances of the arm and leg pieces.

Diagram 2   Diagram 3   Diagram 4

Diagram 5   Diagram 6   Diagram 7

*Order of Appliqué: The most efficient way to appliqué the bear is to begin with the legs and arms. If you prefer to baste the pieces to the background, do so at this time. Thread basting will eliminate the problem of thread catching on pins and will keep the appliqué piece in its proper place. It is easier to handle the appliqué work if you remove the main body piece temporarily. (A big piece with freezer paper inside is not very pliable and may be a hindrance to smooth and comfortable appliquéing of the arms and legs.)

Use appliqué thread in a color to match the arm and leg pieces. Use tiny invisible stitches to secure each piece to the block. The inside edge of the leg does not need to be turned under. It will be covered by the main body piece. The inside and shoulder edges of the arm do not need to be turned under. These areas will be covered by the body and head pieces.

Pins and basting may then be removed. The freezer paper may also be removed by making a small slit (about an inch long) in the background fabric directly behind the appliquéd piece. Do this carefully in order to avoid cutting into the paper, and more important, into the appliqué piece. Use a needle to reach into the opening and loosen the freezer paper from the appliqué piece. With a little tugging, it will come loose and can be removed through the opening. Continue with the appliqué in the following order:

1. Legs
2. Arms
3. Body
4. Ears
5. Head

Note that the main body piece is appliquéd over the inside raw edges

of the legs and arms. The top of the main body does not need to be turned under. The ears are tucked beneath the head piece. Locate and appliqué the outer edges of the ears first. The last piece to be appliquéd is the head. It is placed to cover the raw edges at the top of the main body, the shoulders, and the inside of the ears. After each piece is appliquéd, the pins, basting, and freezer paper may be removed. If you prefer, you may also trim away the excess background fabric behind each appliqué piece. If you choose to do this, do so very carefully in order to avoid cutting into the appliqué piece itself. Trim the background fabric to within ¼" of the appliqué stitching lines.

Appliqué scissors, which have a lip guard to prevent cutting into the appliqué piece, are especially helpful. Removal of the background fabric is recommended if you plan to quilt directly on the appliqué pieces (as in the pictured quilt). Elimination of this extra layer of fabric will make the quilting process easier.

BOWS

After you have completed the 12 bears, make a bow from each of the 12 ribbons. Center these between the body and the head and use the invisible nylon thread to tack them through all layers, as in Diagram 7.

ASSEMBLY

Refer to Diagram 8 for the

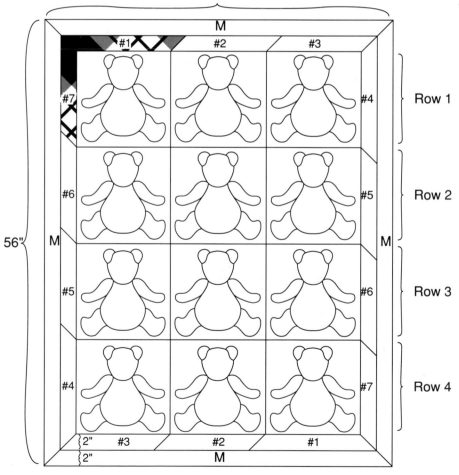

Diagram 8

layout of the Bow Tie Bears quilt. Place the 12 bears in a suitable arrangement of three across and four down. Piece Row 1 by stitching short vertical seams between the blocks, as in Diagram 9. Join the four panels in long horizontal cross seams.

BORDERS

The plaid border is made from pieced bias strips (Templates 6 and 7) that are seamed at the intersections of each bear block. Two sizes are needed, one slightly longer to accommodate the mitered corners. Collect the seven plaid fabrics selected for the pieced border. Designate them numbers 1 through 7 in their order of placement around the quilt, as shown in Diagram 8. Each fabric will be repeated, for a total of 14 pieces in the border. Make a cardboard template of each of the two border pieces (6 and 7). Note

that these templates must be enlarged to the sizes indicated. The stated dimensions do not include seam allowances. These will be added later. Use a protractor to confirm angle accuracy of the enlarged templates. Note and mark the grain lines on each template.

Mark and cut the following pieces from each fabric, adding ¼" seam allowances all around:

Fabric 1: Cut 2 of Template 7
Fabric 2: Cut 2 of Template 6
Fabric 3: Cut 2 of Template 6
Fabric 4: Cut 2 of Template 7
Fabric 5: Cut 2 of Template 6
Fabric 6: Cut 2 of Template 6
Fabric 7: Cut 2 of Template 6

Be careful to note which direction the template is facing when cutting the fabrics. In order to maintain the direction (angles) of the pieced border as pictured, it will be necessary to consistently place the template on the wrong side of

each fabric. This will not be a problem if you are using all woven plaids. In the event of error, you can simply reverse the direction of the angles in the border, or reverse the fabric piece. If you are using some printed plaids (non-reversible fabrics), be especially careful in placing and cutting your border pieces. Arrange the plaid border pieces around the Bow Tie Bears to confirm proper cutting and placement.

CAUTION: Because of the long bias edges, all plaid border pieces must be handled carefully, to avoid stretching. Piece the top border by stitching fabric pieces 1, 2, and 3 together, as shown in Diagram 10. Make a similar panel for the bottom border, as in Diagram 11. The top and bottom borders are actually the same; one is simply inverted.

Next, piece a left-side border by stitching fabric pieces 4, 5, 6, and 7

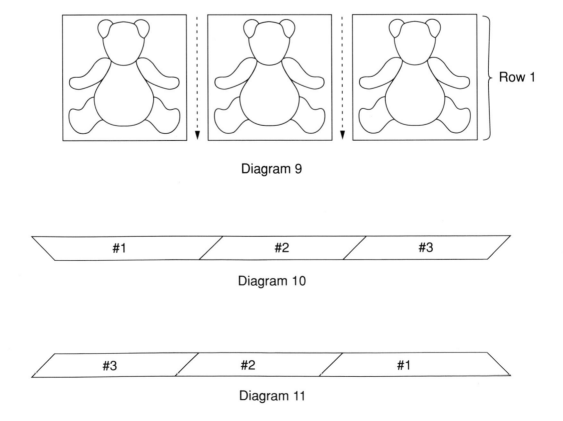

Diagram 9

Diagram 10

Diagram 11

together, as shown in Diagram 12. Make a similar panel for the opposite border, as shown in Diagram 13. Attach the border pieces, taking care not to stretch or distort the bias edges. The seams of the pieced border should be matched and pinned to the seams between the Bear blocks.

Stitch the four borders, mitering the corners. Finally, refer back to Diagram 8 and add the outer 2" muslin borders, mitering the corners.

THE FINISHING TOUCH

QUILTING

Stitch the two reserved muslin backing panels (25" x 60") together in a long seam, as shown in Diagram 14. The finished piece will be about 50" x 60". Place the quilt backing right side down on a large, flat surface. Smooth the batting over it. Place the pressed quilt top over the batting, right side up. Pin or thread-baste the three layers together for quilting. Use a washable marking pencil or soap chip to mark the quilting lines suggested on page 124. Use natural-color thread.

• Quilt around the edge of each appliqué piece.

• Quilt ¼" from the edge on each arm, leg, and ear.

• Quilt the curved shapes inside the main body piece, as shown in Diagram 15.

• Quilt facial lines as shown in Diagram 16.

• Quilt diagonal crosshatch lines at 2" intervals, on the background muslin, as suggested in the photograph.

• Quilt a gently curving line to join each bear hand-in-hand with its neighbor(s).

BINDING

Trim the batting to ½" larger than the quilt top, to allow for filler in the binding. Trim the backing to match the top. From the one yard of teal binding fabric, make 3" wide continuous bias strips. Fold the binding in half lengthwise, wrong sides together. Then attach it to the quilt front in a seam that penetrates all the layers. Turn the binding to the back and whipstitch it in place.

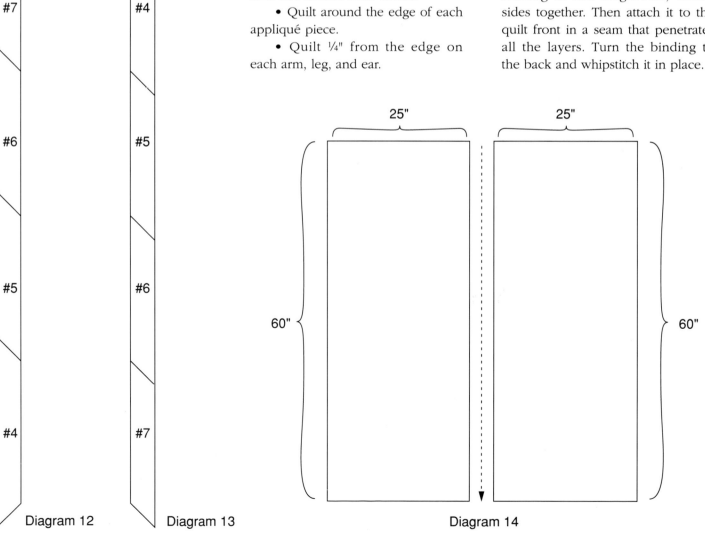

Diagram 12   Diagram 13   Diagram 14

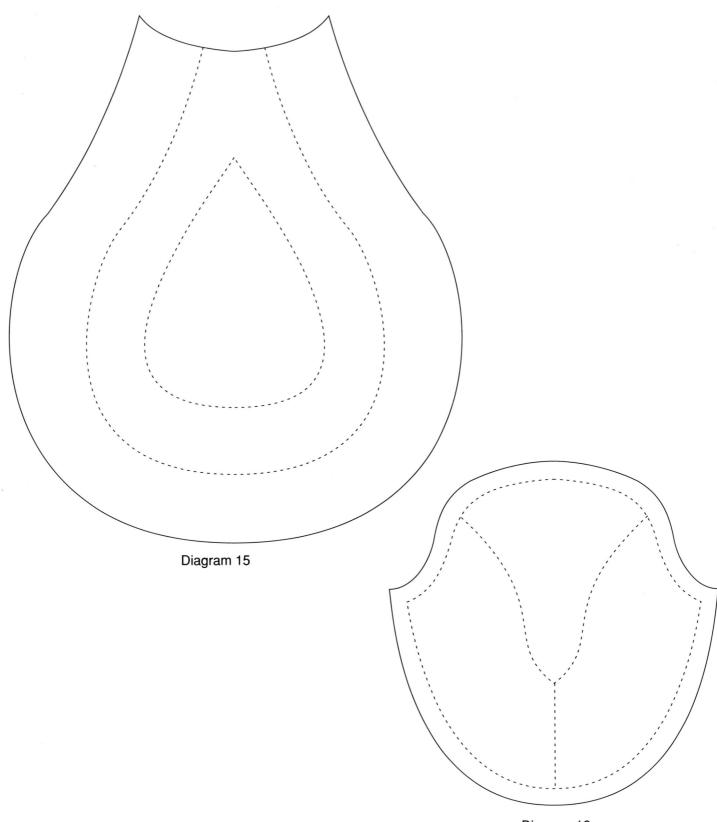

Diagram 15

Diagram 16

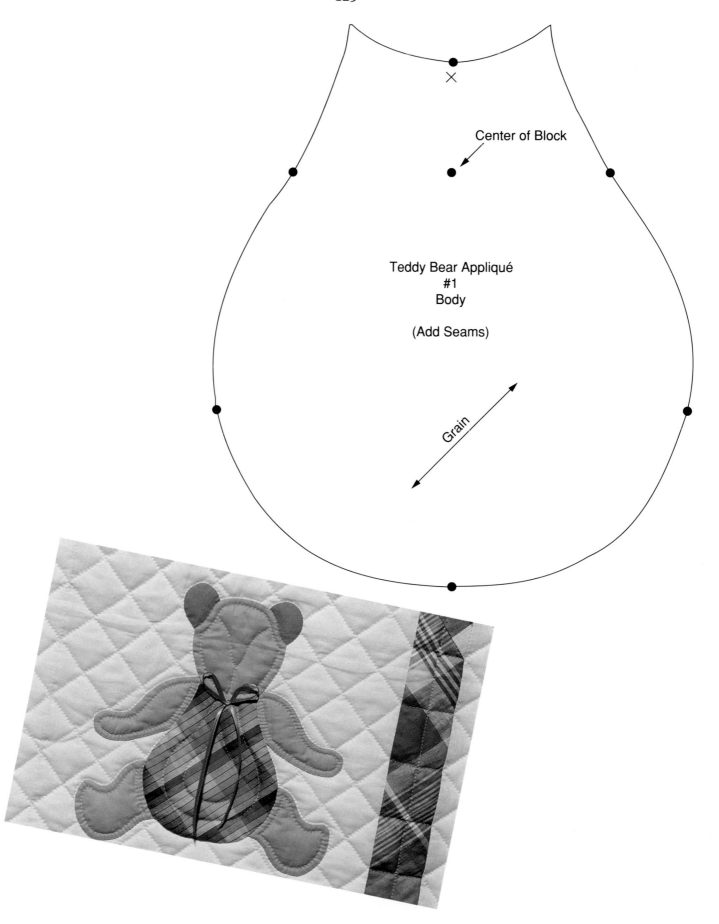

Center of Block

Teddy Bear Appliqué
#1
Body

(Add Seams)

Grain

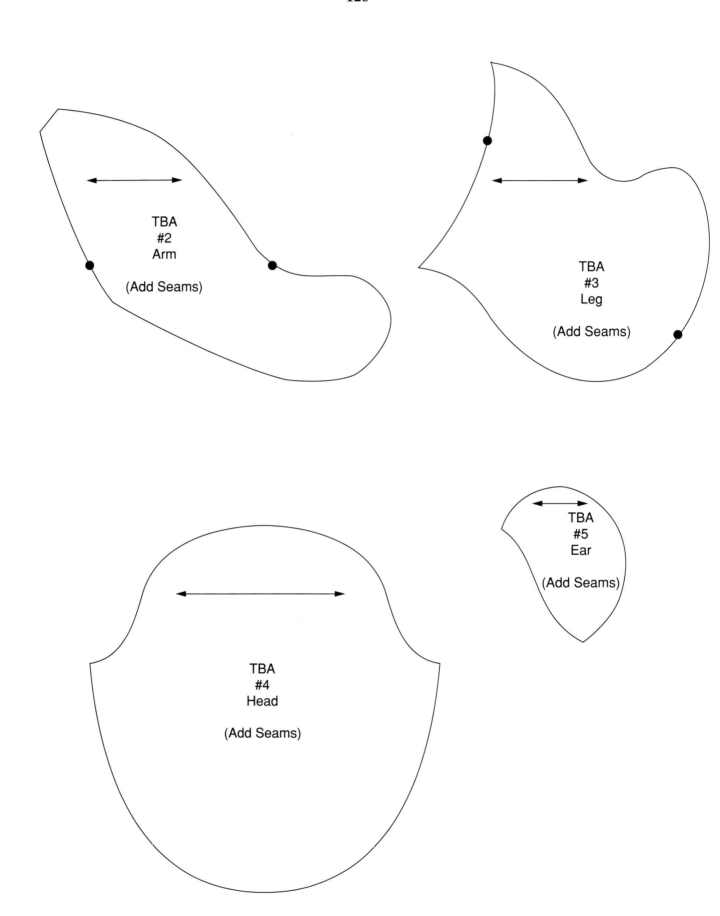

TBA
#2
Arm

(Add Seams)

TBA
#3
Leg

(Add Seams)

TBA
#5
Ear

(Add Seams)

TBA
#4
Head

(Add Seams)

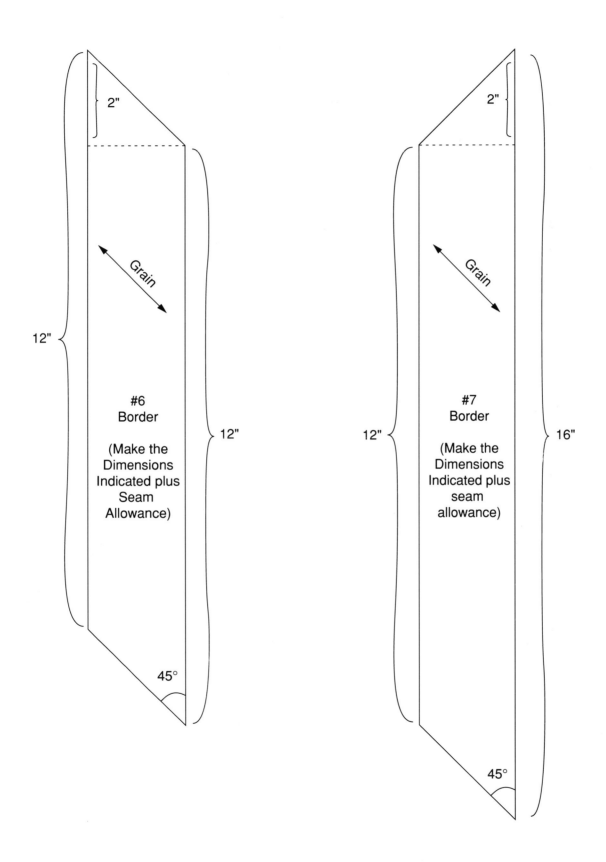

2"

Grain

12"

12"

#6
Border

(Make the
Dimensions
Indicated plus
Seam
Allowance)

45°

2"

Grain

12"

16"

#7
Border

(Make the
Dimensions
Indicated plus
seam
allowance)

45°

EXTRA FANCY U.S. NO. 1
(RICE SACK QUILT)
Quilt by the Author

EXTRA FANCY U.S. NO. 1

(Portions of the Rice Sack story first appeared in Quilting Today *magazine, and are reprinted here with the kind permission of Patti Bachelder, editor.)*

Cloth sacks and bags have been an important resource for quilters for the past century. Sacks were usually washed repeatedly with homemade lye soap, scrubbed on a washboard to remove the manufacturer's printing, then dyed for use as quilt backs. Some quilters patched over the brand names in an effort to disguise them. One Ohio quiltmaker, the daughter of a feed-store owner, took exception, proudly displaying her father's fertilizer bags and company name on her quilt.

A Tennessee quilter used chicken-feed bags in her "hard times" quilt, which was finished during the depression, when families economized in every way possible. Women made use of the cloth from the 100-pound bags of feed. When empty, the bags were washed and made into quilt linings, sheets, and pillowcases. The "hard times" quilt is backed with a chicken feed-sack lining.

My research has revealed several kinds of bags and sacks that may have been used for quilts. They can be grouped in several categories:

• Bags from food for human consumption: flour, salt, sugar, rice, oatmeal and other grains and cereals, potatoes.

• Bags from food for animal consumption: hog chow, mule and horse feed, dairy-cow feed, hen-laying mash, chicken feed, etc.

• Bags from farm-related goods and products: seeds (corn, oats, soybeans, alfalfa), fertilizer, tobacco, wool.

• Miscellaneous Bags: money, sand, gravel, and lead shot.

My interest in the use of bags and sacks was inspired by my grandmother's collection of sacks and by my friend Alice Weickelt, who has been making quilts from rice bags. Alice is a teacher of English as a second language for elementary-age children from the Hmong refugee families in our Eau Claire community. In an attempt to relate better to her students, she used several quilts in her class, including one with parts made from old flour sacks. One Hmong girl asked, "If you can use flour sacks, can you use rice bags?" And that was the beginning of a new line of quiltmaking for Alice.

Her students brought samples of the 100-pound sacks in which the Hmong families buy rice. Alice incorporated the various emblems and printed information into a quilt top. For quilting in the alternate blocks, Alice asked her students to draw pictures of various implements used in planting, harvesting, and preparing the rice. She hand quilted these designs – a basket, a knife, an ax, a rice huller, a hoe, and a crossbow – in the plain blocks.

Alice still has that first quilt, and has continued to make several others, which she gives to new refugee families as they arrive in the community, or to their newborn babies. These quilts are simply designed with strips of colored cloth between the blocks, tied, and presented to families as needed. Her rice-bag projects reflect a total of over 5,000 pounds of rice, and she expects to continue making quilts as long as the rice is available in cloth bags.

Inspired by my family's collection of sacks and Alice's rice-bag quilts, I designed a quilt with recycled rice bags. I call it EXTRA FANCY U.S. NO. 1. It features six bag styles with colorful red and yellow emblems – a giant white crane against a red sun; large yellow roses and shields with swords and drums; red plum flowers, and a Pacific coastal scene. Trade names and printed information appear in English, Japanese, and Chinese characters.

I followed an ordinary design and construction process. First I opened the seams of the bags. Then I washed them to remove traces of food and to soften the colors. The front of a 100-pound bag yielded a panel about 15" x 30", a 25-pound bag a panel about 12" x 18".

Panels were pieced directly to each other with "filler" material such as printed nutritional information and cooking instructions taken from the backs of the bags. I selected a dual border of red and yellow and a dark blue binding to reflect the colorful center designs. EXTRA FANCY U.S. NO. 1 is hand-quilted with a background of diagonal parallel lines about 1½" apart. The six emblem designs are quilted to enhance the shapes and letters.

For some people, EXTRA FANCY U.S. NO. 1 will evoke memories of a time when thrifty women dismantled bags and reused them in quilts and household necessities. They called it "making do." Today we call it recycling.

Another rice-sack quilt with cranes and red shield designs is featured in my book, A Collection of Favorite Quilts: Narratives, Directions, and Patterns for 15 Quilts.

For information about ordering new rice bags, send a large SASE to Quilt Enterprises, 6921 Timber Ridge Circle, Eau Claire, WI 54701.

EXTRA FANCY U.S. NO. 1

FOR STARTERS

The following list will help you enjoy a smooth start and steady progress in your work on the Rice Bag quilt. It contains a variety of general information about making the quilt:

- Information for ordering rice sacks is available by sending a large SASE to Quilt Enterprises, 6921 Timber Ridge Circle, Eau Claire, WI 54701.
- Six bags of various sizes and styles are used in the photographed quilt.
- Bags should be washed gently by hand to remove soil and excess dyes.
- Wash and press all other fabrics before you begin cutting.
- All seams are ¼".
- No templates are required.
- The inner red border is 2" wide.
- The outer yellow border is 3" wide.
- The binding is dark blue.
- The finished size for Extra Fancy

U.S. No. 1 is 58" x 74".

NOTE: The photographed quilt varies slightly from the measurements in the directions and diagrams.

SUPPLIES

Use 44"/45" cotton.

Fabric:

Red (solid): 2 yards

Yellow (solid or fine print): 2¼ yards

Bags: You will need six large (25 lb. or 100 lb.) muslin bags. An address for a mail-order source is listed on page 129. Twenty-five lb. bags can be pieced with additional fabric from the backs of larger bags.

Binding: 1 yard of Dark Blue.

Backing: 4¼ yards of good quality unbleached muslin.

Batting: Use a 72" x 90" (twin size) bonded polyester batt.

OTHER SUPPLIES

- Iron

- Marking pencils or soap chips
- Scissors (for paper and fabric)
- Rulers
- Large 45/90-degree triangle
- Thread for piecing
- Pins
- Thread or safety pins for basting
- Quilting needles
- Two spools natural-color quilting thread
- Thimble
- Long straightedge
- Hoop or frame for quilting

READY TO WORK

BAG PANELS

Begin by opening the seams in each bag. Then wash gently in warm soapy water to remove sizing, soil, and excess dye. Press each bag.

Measure the large bags. If the front panel of a bag measures at least 17" x 33", it can be used intact. Lay each large bag on a flat surface (a large cutting mat works well). Locate the center of the front panel on each bag. Measure from side to side and top to bottom to mark a panel 16½" x 32½" (seams included), as shown in Diagram 1. Use a 45/90-degree large triangle to check for accuracy in the corners. Be sure that all edges are parallel.

Cut out each large bag panel.

For small bags with front panels that measure less than 17" x 33", you will need to add some "filler" muslin from the back of the small bag or from the backs of the larger bags, to achieve the desired panel size. The photographed quilt includes two small (25 lb.) bags (in the upper right and upper left corners of the quilt). These two bags were enlarged by adding some printed sections (nutritional information and cooking instructions) and long muslin strips from other large bag backs.

Lay each small bag on a flat surface and locate the center of the

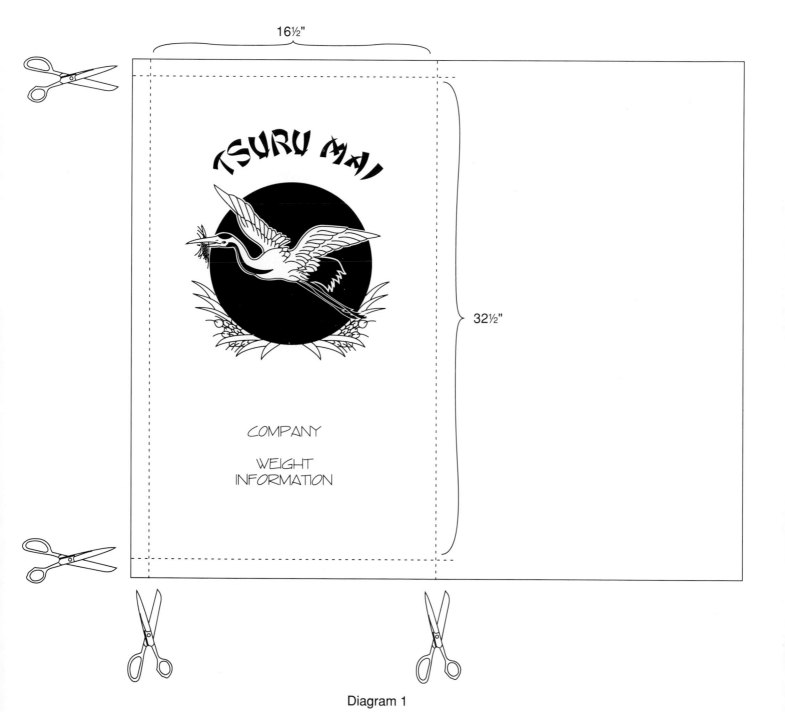

Diagram 1

front panel. Using the large triangle and long straightedge, mark and cut a front panel as large as the bag will allow. Then cut sections from the other bag backs to make a finished panel that measures 16½" by 32½" (with seams included). An example of a "pieced" panel is shown in Diagram 2.

You will need a total of six, 16½" x 32½" panels for the quilt.

BORDERS

Cut the following pieces from the Red fabric (allowances for seams and mitering included):

Cut two side borders 2½" x 68½".

Cut two end borders 2½" x 52½".

Cut the following pieces from the Yellow fabric (allowances for seams and mitering included):

Cut two side borders 3½" x 74½".

Cut two end borders 3½" x 58½".

ASSEMBLY

Refer to Diagram 3 for the general quilt layout. Begin assembly by piecing the three bags in the upper half of the quilt (Bags #1, 2, and 3) in ¼" seams, as in Diagram 4.

Then piece the three lower bags (#4, 5, and 6) in the lower half. Stitch the two sections together in a cross seam.

Next, attach the inner Red (2") borders, mitering the corners. Add the outer Yellow (3") borders to complete the quilt top.

THE FINISHING TOUCH

QUILTING

From the 4¼ yards of muslin backing fabric, cut two 2⅛ yard lengths. Keep one intact (about 42" wide). From the other piece, cut two 12" widths. Join a 12" width to each side of the intact center panel. Press seams toward the outside.

Place the quilt backing right side down on a large, flat surface. Smooth the batting over it. Place the pressed quilt top over the batting, right side up. Pin or thread-baste the three layers together for quilting.

Use a washable marking pencil, a large triangle, and a long straightedge to mark the "hanging diamonds" quilting suggested in Diagram 5.

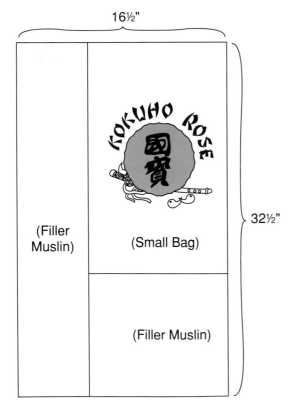

Diagram 2

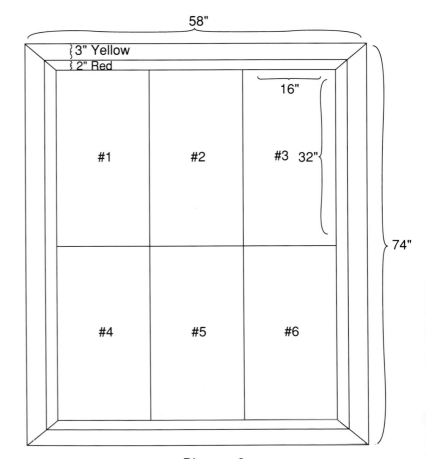

Diagram 3

The diagonal lines are marked at 2" intervals. Use a long ruler and pins to locate the 2" intervals along the sides, top, and bottom of each bag panel. Mark the diagonal parallel lines and quilt, using natural-color quilting thread.

Highlight the printed design areas of each bag with additional quilting around the shapes (such as the crane, sun, shield, sword, boat scene, and grains of rice). Outline quilt around the shapes and fill in the larger emblems (shield, sun, and crane) with quilted concentric circles.

BINDING

Trim the batting to ½" larger than the quilt top, to allow for filler in the binding. Trim the backing to match the top. From the one yard of dark blue binding fabric, make 3" wide continuous bias binding.

Fold the binding in half lengthwise, wrong sides together. Then attach it to the quilt front in a seam that penetrates all the layers. Turn the binding to the back and whipstitch it in place.

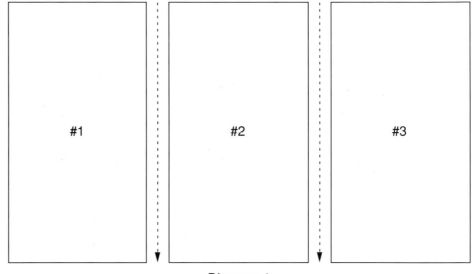

Diagram 4

Diagram 5

IROQUOIS
(NATIVE AMERICAN QUILT)
Quilt by the Author

IROQUOIS

(Portions of the Iroquois story first appeared in Quilting Today *magazine, and are included here with the kind permission of Patti Bachelder, editor.)*

The IROQUOIS quilt has been a favorite wherever it has been displayed or juried. Blue ribbons, Viewer's Choice awards, and invitational showings have all been part of its past. Whether hung in quilt shows, in international festivals, in classrooms, or in the privacy of our home, it has attracted viewers with numerous questions and comments.

IROQUOIS is a family favorite, as well. Of all the quilts that have passed through my quilt frame vying for a place on a bed or wall, IROQUOIS has been the all-time winner, frequently hanging in our dining room. From time to time it is taken down and put into temporary storage, but it always seems to make its way back to the wall again after a few weeks.

Why is IROQUOIS attractive to viewers and quilters?

Three reasons come to mind: The medallion-style setting, the color combinations, and the unique designs.

The medallion-style was regaining popularity in the early 1980's. It was a welcome relief to the confines of strictly traditional patterns and block-by-block construction. Freedom to explore beyond the block inspired many quiltmakers and designers to experiment with less usual settings like the medallion. A whole new style and genre of quilts began to appear as medallion quilts captured attention.

Also, viewers liked the blue/brown/beige color combination that became so popular a few years ago. The mixture of natural colors, of earth and sky, is very satisfying. Soft, natural tones blend comfortably with a touch of blue.

Finally, IROQUOIS intrigues viewers with its designs. Both traditional shapes and new and unusual designs are included. This sharp contrast of the familiar and the novel is captivating.

IROQUOIS is also my personal favorite for a couple of reasons. First, it was made for my son, Matt, who is a member of the Oneida Tribe of Wisconsin Indians (one of the Iroquois Nations). This work is also my first attempt to design and construct a quilt from "scratch" with nobody's suggestions or restrictions to guide or confine the process.

I made IROQUOIS at a point in my quiltmaking when I had more than enough quilts to cover all the beds in our home. My husband had been encouraging me to design a special quilt for Matt, a quilt that would reflect his Native American background. It was time to try.

Gathering up my courage, I researched several Iroquois and Oneida design and craft books. I also read folk tales and creation accounts and studied the history of the Oneida Tribe and the Iroquois Nation. After accumulating a file of ideas and designs pertinent to Matt's background, I pondered how to adapt and incorporate them into fabric.

I settled on two principal design ideas: the Iroquois creation account, and the historical Wampum Treaty Belts. Specific designs included the Primal Turtle, the Great Earth Tree, the Celestial Sun, the Evergrowing Tree, Wampum Shells, and Quillwork.

Centermost in the IROQUOIS quilt is the "Primal Turtle" (or World Turtle) and the '"Great Earth Tree." The mythological turtle is a clan figure and is frequently used in Iroquois designs. In tribal accounts, "the earth was formed atop a piece of mud on the back of a turtle that had returned from the depths of the sea. The roots of the "Great Earth Tree" were believed to penetrate down into the Primal Turtle's back.

Several Iroquois tribes express peace through the metaphor of a tree whose top they say will reach the sun and whose branches, which afford shelter and repose, extend a great distance. That tree was variously known to the confederacy as "the Evergrowing Tree, the World Tree, the Great Earth Tree, the Tree of Life, the Tree of Peace, and the Celestial Tree. It was thought to stand at the center of the world, bearing the sun and moon aloft in its branches."

The celestial sun at the top of the tree recalls the use of the circle, among the oldest of designs used in Iroquois crafts. The circle was regarded as "a symbol of life, its unbroken circumference being significant of the continuation of life in the world beyond."

The outer pieced border (blue hexagonal shapes against a brown background) is based on one of several Iroquois wampum treaty belts that date from the late sixteenth and early seventeenth centuries. Wampum treaty belts incorporated many designs – hexagons, diamonds, overlapping triangles, crosses, diagonal lines or bars, circles, hearts, pipes, houses, human and animal figures. Designs were arranged in symbolic patterns. Their meaning was given by the belt's maker or was said to have been "talked into it" when the treaty was made. Thus, design stories serve as reminders of tribal events, of the ratification of treaties, and to guarantee proposals made between people.

A belt known as the "Wing" or "Dust Fan of the Council President Belt" was the inspiration for my quilt border. The belt features a series of ten connecting six-sided figures on a white background. That design is said "to represent the Evergrowing Tree, which by its repetition symbolizes the permanence and continuous growth of the Great League of the Iroquois." This belt was displayed whenever the constitution of the Six Nations was recited.

The "Evergrowing Tree" design appears on all four borders of the IROQUOIS quilt. The top and bottom have the ten hexagons that read from the center in both directions.

Corner stars (large and small) represent the Celestial Stars. The pattern is a familiar Four-Patch known to quiltmakers variously as Rising Star or Star and Squares.

The "shell" quilting pattern behind the turtle reflects the use of wampum beads. These small cylindrical shell beads were made from various species of shells. Those used in Iroquois treaty belts were often cut from the common hard-shell clam. In addition to their use as necklaces and for purposes of exchange, shell beads were used in public transactions of various nature, and to convey or record a design idea or thought.

Decorative quilting, adapted from an Iroquois quill design, is seen in the light-colored triangles surrounding the central medallion. Quill embroidery frequently featured curved and floral designs and was used in leggings, moccasins, skirts, and bags. My design was modified slightly to fit the background shape.

IROQUOIS is a culmination of my efforts to combine significant designs from Matt's tribal heritage with my quiltmaking passion. The research and design processes were challenging, and project execution was a pleasure. The outcome was very gratifying for all the members of our family.

IROQUOIS is now in temporary storage. We bring it out for occasional family use, special events, and invitational shows. Mostly it is set aside for safe-keeping so Matt can have the quilt for his own use and pleasure during his lifetime.

IROQUOIS

NOTE: Instructions for the Iroquois quilt (66" x 84") are a departure from the format used for other quilts in this book. Directions include four piecing and quilting designs that have general appeal. Four shapes and designs that can be easily adapted or incorporated into other quilt projects are as follows:

- The Rising Star (pieced block)
- The Evergrowing Tree (pieced border)
- The Floral Quillwork Design (decorative quilting)
- The Clam Shell Design (background quilting)

Details regarding fabric amounts, color, and specific instructions for the specialized appliqué and other details are NOT included.

A. RISING STAR BLOCK (10" square, finished)

Color Key:
R = Dark Brown Print
L = Light Print
B = Blue Print
C = Cream

Refer to Diagram 1 for an illustration of the Rising Star block.

Begin by making templates of the five Rising Star pattern pieces (Templates 1, 2, 3, 4, 5, and 6). Mark the grain lines on each template. Note that ¼" seams must be added on all sides of each piece. Cut the following pieces:

Template 1: Cut four Light
Template 2: Cut eight Brown
Template 3: Cut four Light
Template 4: Cut eight Blue
Template 5: Cut four Cream
Template 6: Cut one Brown and four Cream

Collect the 33 pieces that make up a block. Arrange the pieces right side up on a flat surface, according

to Diagram 2. Use the following steps to piece the star:

Stitch small Brown (R) triangles to the short sides of the larger Light triangle (L), as shown in Diagram 3. Make four of these units.

Add a Light (L) square on each end of two of these units, as shown in Diagram 4.

Stitch a large Brown (R) square between the two remaining units, as shown in Diagram 5.

Join the three units in horizontal seams, as shown in Diagram 6. (Note: This portion of the block, as shown in Diagram 7 (page 138), is similar to the stars used in the corners of the Iroquois pieced border.)

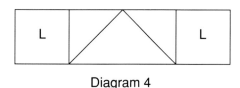

Diagram 3

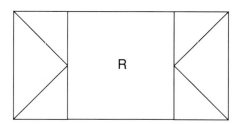

Diagram 4

Diagram 1

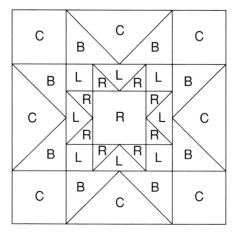

Diagram 2

Diagram 5

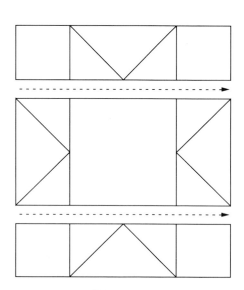

Diagram 6

Diagram 7

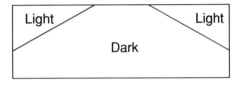

Diagram 8

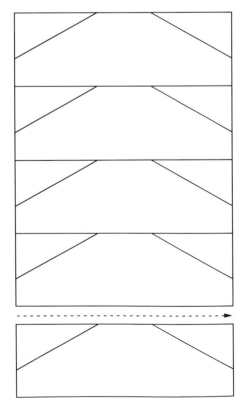

Diagram 9

To complete the outer portion of the star, piece the Blue (B) and Cream (C) pieces in steps similar to Diagrams 3 through 6.

B. EVERGROWING TREE
(6" pieced border)

Make templates of the two Evergrowing Tree pattern pieces, Templates 7 (elongated hexagon) and 8 (triangle). Be sure to note the grain lines and add seam allowances.

Select a dark color for the hexagons and a light color for the background triangles.

Stitch small triangles on each side of the hexagon, to form a rectangle, as in Diagram 8. Make enough to cover the desired border length.

Stitch the rectangles together as is suggested in Diagram 9. A finished border sample is shown below in Diagram 10.

C. FLORAL QUILTING DESIGN
(decorative quilting)

A variety of quilting styles were used on the Iroquois quilt. Decorative quilting is used on the large muslin triangles around the turtle medallion. This floral motif (Design A, page 140) was adapted from decorative Iroquois quillwork.

Mark the design on selected triangles. (A right triangle about 10" on the short side is about the right size.) Two designs set back-to-back will fit a 10"-12" square nicely.

D. CLAM SHELL DESIGN
(background quilting)

"Shell" filler quilting (Design B, page 141) is used in the territory behind the turtle. "Shell" quilting recalls the use of cylindrical beads (cut from the common hard-shell clam) in the early Iroquois treaty belts.

Diagram 10

Rising Star
#1

(Add ¼" seams)

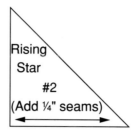

Rising
Star
#2
(Add ¼" seams)

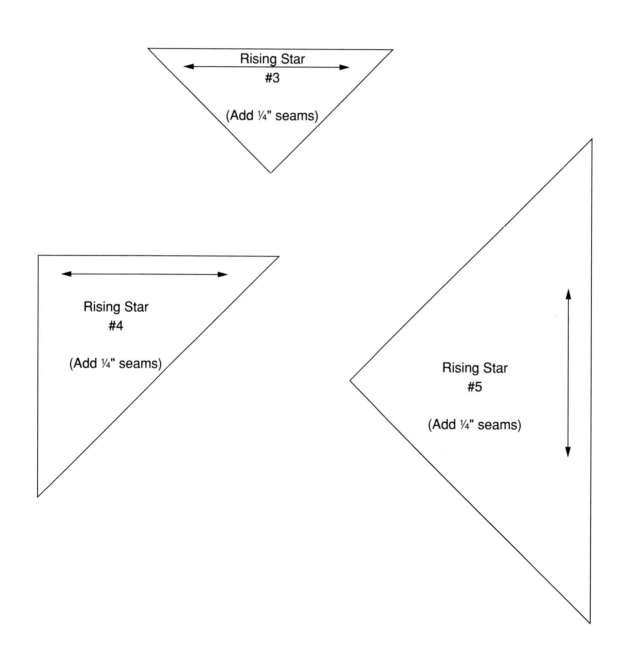

Rising Star
#3

(Add ¼" seams)

Rising Star
#4

(Add ¼" seams)

Rising Star
#5

(Add ¼" seams)

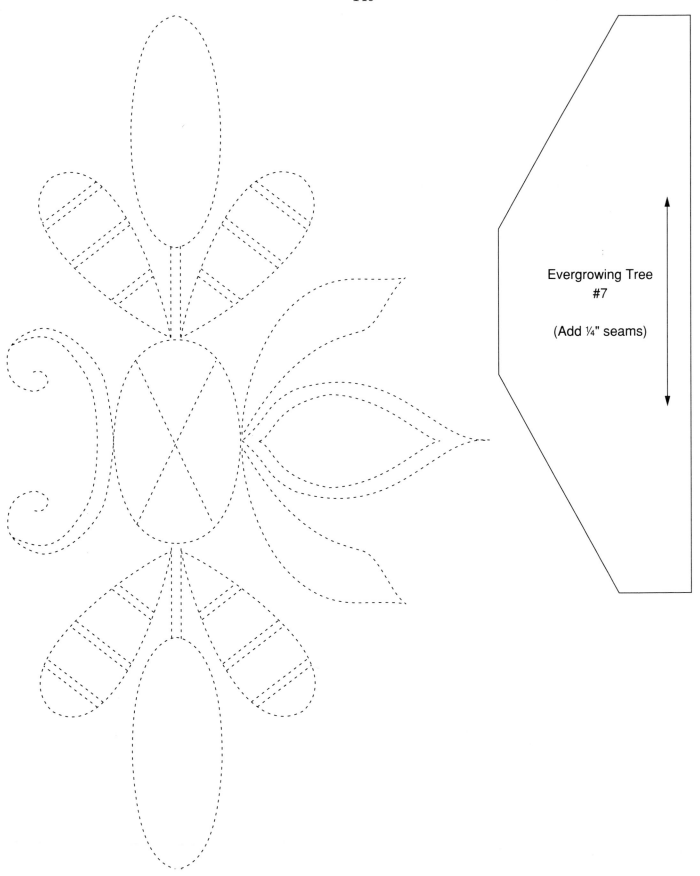

Evergrowing Tree
#7

(Add ¼" seams)

Quilting Design A

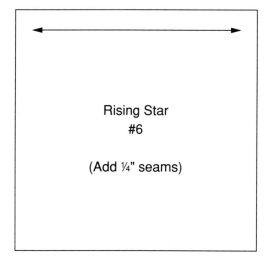

Rising Star
#6

(Add ¼" seams)

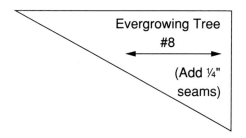

Evergrowing Tree
#8

(Add ¼" seams)

Quilting Design B

DESIGN WORKSHEETS FOR SELECTED QUILT PATTERNS

1. Virginia Reel

2. Cubic Plaids (Square-in-Square)

3. Evening Star (Four-Patch Star)

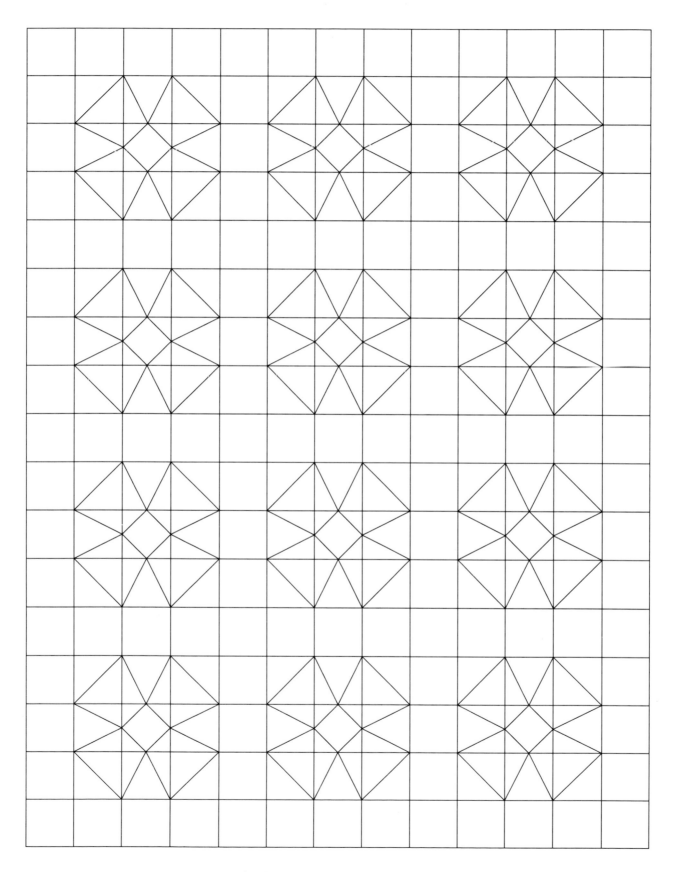

4. Blue Medley (Nine-Patch Star)

5. Mexican Star

6. Texas Stars (Eight-Point Star)

7. Log Cabin

8. Spools

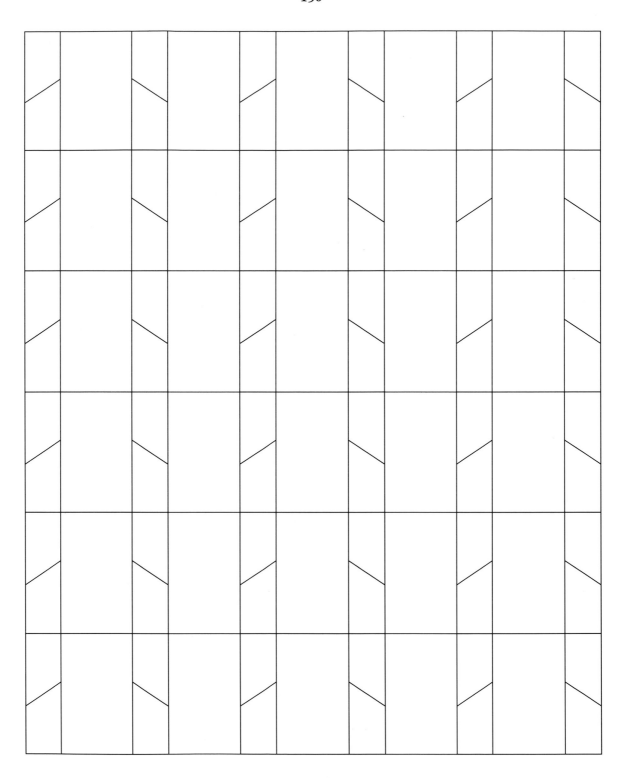

9. Mixed T

BIBLIOGRAPHY

Florence, Judy. AWARD-WINNING QUICK QUILTS. Lombard, Illinois: Wallace-Homestead Book Company, 1988.
Features projects that can be completed quickly with tandem piecing and quick cutting techniques. Also contains numerous original designs for hand-quilting.

Florence, Judy. AWARD-WINNING SCRAP QUILTS. Lombard, Illinois: Wallace-Homestead Book Company, 1987.
Instructions for converting fabric remnants into striking designs. Supply lists and detailed approaches to help you get started. Diagrams, templates, and photographs to help you use leftover fabric to good advantage.

Florence, Judy. A COLLECTION OF FAVORITE QUILTS: NARRATIVES, DIRECTIONS, AND PATTERNS FOR 15 QUILTS. Paducah, Kentucky: American Quilter's Society, 1990.
Both traditional and innovative designs are included, with full-page color photographs of each quilt, plus 50 additional color detail photographs. Extensive information about fabrics, supplies, and construction, plus a captivating story about each quilt.

Hertzberg, Hazel W., American Anthropological Association. THE GREAT TREE AND THE LONGHOUSE. New York: The MacMillan Company, 1966.
The culture of the Iroquois Nation, including the creation myth, kinship and family, the founding of the confederacy, and recent history.

Horton, Roberta. PLAIDS & STRIPES: THE USE OF DIRECTIONAL FABRIC IN QUILTS. Layfayette, California: C & T Publishing, 1990.
Ideas and ways to use plaids and stripes to create more exciting quilts, including traditional, Log Cabin, utility, African-American, appliqué, and contemporary quilts.

Laury, Jean Ray and California Heritage Quilt Project. HO FOR CALIFORNIA! PIONEER WOMEN AND THEIR QUILTS. New York: E. P. Dutton, 1990.
A book about quilts and the women who made them. One hundred and one quilts documented in color photographs with thought-provoking personal chronicles of the quiltmakers.

Lyford, Carrie A. IROQUOIS CRAFTS. Stevens Point, Wisconsin: R. Schneider, Publishers, 1982.
An interesting and useful collection of the material culture of the Iroquois, with descriptions of how they were made and used in everyday life.

McKim, Ruby. 101 PATCHWORK PATTERNS. New York: Dover Publications, Inc., 1962.
Quilt name stories, cutting designs, material suggestions, yardage estimates, step-by-step instructions for over 100 popular patterns. Originally published in 1931, it is still a great reference.

Penders, Mary Coyne. COLOR AND CLOTH: THE QUILTMAKER'S ULTIMATE WORKBOOK. San Francisco: The Quilt Digest Press, 1989.
A thorough color theory workbook with a series of hands-on exercises to help you translate your color choices to fabric selection. Excellent photographs and diagrams.

QUILTER'S NEWSLETTER MAGAZINE, March 1990, Wheatridge, CO: Leman Publications, Inc.
Jean Ray Laury's quotes on pages 6 and 8 were first published in the March 1990 issue.

QUILTING TODAY Magazine. Patti Bachelder, Editor. New Milford, Pennsylvania: Chitra Publications.
See Issues #17, #18, and #19 respectively for articles on rice bag quilts, using plaids in quilts, and incorporating ethnic designs in quilts.

Tehanetorens. TALES OF THE IROQUOIS. Rooseveltown, New York: Akwesasne Notes (Mohawk Nation), 1976.
Stories to provide us with another way to see the world, teaching us the history of this land and the proper way for human beings to live together.

~American Quilter's Society~
dedicated to publishing books for today's quilters

The following AQS publications are currently available:

- **Adapting Architectural Details for Quilts,** Carol Wagner, #2282: AQS, 1991, 88 pages, softbound, $12.95
- **American Beauties: Rose & Tulip Quilts,** Gwen Marston & Joe Cunningham, #1907: AQS, 1988, 96 pages, softbound, $14.95
- **America's Pictorial Quilts,** Caron L. Mosey, #1662: AQS, 1985, 112 pages, hardbound, $19.95
- **Applique Designs: My Mother Taught Me to Sew,** Faye Anderson, #2121: AQS, 1990, 80 pages, softbound, $12.95
- **Arkansas Quilts: Arkansas Warmth,** Arkansas Quilter's Guild, Inc., #1908: AQS, 1987, 144 pages, hardbound, $24.95
- **The Art of Hand Applique,** Laura Lee Fritz, #2122: AQS, 1990, 80 pages, softbound, $14.95
- **...Ask Helen More About Quilting Designs,** Helen Squire, #2099: AQS, 1990, 54 pages, 17 x 11, spiral-bound, $14.95
- **Award-Winning Quilts & Their Makers: Vol. I, The Best of AQS Shows – 1985-1987,** #2207: AQS, 1991, 232 pages, softbound, $24.95
- **Award-Winning Quilts & Their Makers: Vol. II, The Best of AQS Shows – 1988-1989,** #2354: AQS, 1992, 176 pages, softbound, $24.95
- **Classic Basket Quilts,** Elizabeth Porter & Marianne Fons, #2208: AQS, 1991, 128 pages, softbound, $16.95
- **A Collection of Favorite Quilts,** Judy Florence, #2119: AQS, 1990, 136 pages, softbound, $18.95
- **Creative Machine Art,** Sharee Dawn Roberts, #2355: AQS, 1992, 139 pages, softbound, $24.95
- **Dear Helen, Can You Tell Me?...all about quilting designs,** Helen Squire, #1820: AQS, 1987, 56 pages, 17 x 11, spiral-bound, $12.95
- **Dyeing & Overdyeing of Cotton Fabrics,** Judy Mercer Tescher, #2030: AQS, 1990, 54 pages, softbound, $9.95
- **Flavor Quilts for Kids to Make: Complete Instructions for Teaching Children to Dye, Decorate & Sew Quilts,** Jennifer Amor #2356: AQS, 1991, 120 pages, softbound, $12.95
- **From Basics to Binding: A Complete Guide to Making Quilts,** Karen Kay Buckley, #2381: AQS, 1992, 160 pages, softbound, $16.95
- **Fun & Fancy Machine Quiltmaking,** Lois Smith, #1982: AQS, 1989, 144 pages, softbound, $19.95
- **Gallery of American Quilts: 1849-1988,** #1938: AQS, 1988, 128 pages, softbound, $19.95
- **Gallery of American Quilts 1860-1989: Book II,** #2129: AQS, 1990, 128 pages, softbound, $19.95
- **The Grand Finale: A Quilter's Guide to Finishing Projects,** Linda Denner, #1924: AQS, 1988, 96 pages, softbound, $14.95
- **Heirloom Miniatures,** Tina M. Gravatt, #2097: AQS, 1990, 64 pages, softbound, $9.95
- **Home Study Course in Quiltmaking,** Jeannie M. Spears, #2031: AQS, 1990, 240 pages, softbound, $19.95
- **Infinite Stars,** Gayle Bong, #2283: AQS, 1992, 72 pages, softbound, $12.95
- **The Ins and Outs: Perfecting the Quilting Stitch,** Patricia J. Morris, #2120: AQS, 1990, 96 pages, softbound, $9.95
- **Irish Chain Quilts: A Workbook of Irish Chains & Related Patterns,** Joyce B. Peaden, #1906: AQS, 1988, 96 pages, softbound, $14.95
- **The Log Cabin Returns to Kentucky: Quilts from the Pilgrim/Roy Collection,** Gerald Roy and Paul Pilgrim, #3329: AQS, 1992, 36 pages, softbound, $12.95
- **Marbling Fabrics for Quilts: A Guide for Learning & Teaching,** Kathy Fawcett & Carol Shoaf, #2206: AQS, 1991, 72 pages, softbound, $12.95
- **Missouri Heritage Quilts,** Bettina Havig, #1718: AQS, 1986, 104 pages, softbound, $14.95
- **Nancy Crow: Quilts and Influences,** Nancy Crow, #1981: AQS, 1990, 256 pages, hardcover, $29.95
- **Nancy Crow: Work in Transition,** Nancy Crow, #3331: AQS, 1992, 32 pages, softbound, $12.95
- **No Dragons on My Quilt,** Jean Ray Laury with Ritva Laury & Lizabeth Laury, #2153: AQS, 1990, 52 pages, hardcover, $12.95
- **Oklahoma Heritage Quilts,** Oklahoma Quilt Heritage Project #2032: AQS, 1990, 144 pages, softbound, $19.95
- **Quilt Groups Today: Who They Are, Where They Meet, What They Do, and How to Contact Them; A Complete Guide for 1992-1993,** #3308: AQS, 1992, 336 pages, softbound $14.95
- **Quiltmaker's Guide: Basics & Beyond,** Carol Doak, #2284: AQS, 1992, 208 pages, softbound, $19.95
- **Quilts: The Permanent Collection – MAQS,** #2257: AQS, 1991, 100 pages, 10 x 6½, softbound, $9.95
- **Scarlet Ribbons: American Indian Technique for Today's Quilters,** Helen Kelley, #1819: AQS, 1987, 104 pages, softbound, $15.95
- **Sensational Scrap Quilts,** Darra Duffy Williamson, #2357: AQS, 1992, 152 pages, softbound, $24.95
- **Sets & Borders,** Gwen Marston & Joe Cunningham, #1821: AQS, 1987, 104 pages, softbound, $14.95
- **Somewhere in Between: Quilts and Quilters of Illinois,** Rita Barrow Barber, #1790: AQS, 1986, 78 pages, softbound, $14.95
- **Stenciled Quilts for Christmas,** Marie Monteith Sturmer, #2098: AQS, 1990, 104 pages, softbound, $14.95
- **Texas Quilts – Texas Treasures,** Texas Heritage Quilt Society, #1760: AQS, 1986, 160 pages, hardbound, $24.95
- **A Treasury of Quilting Designs,** Linda Goodmon Emery, #2029: AQS, 1990, 80 pages, 14 x 11, spiral-bound, $14.95
- **Wonderful Wearables: A Celebration of Creative Clothing,** Virginia Avery, #2286: AQS, 1991, 184 pages, softbound, $24.95

These books can be found in local bookstores and quilt shops. If you are unable to locate a title in your area, you can order by mail from AQS, P.O. Box 3290, Paducah, KY 42002-3290. Please add $1 for the first book and 40¢ for each additional one to cover postage and handling. (International orders, please add $1.50 for the first book and $1.00 for each additional book.)